DEVOTIONS FOR KIDS

A PILE OF STONES

JESSIE SCHUT

CRC Publications
Grand Rapids, Michigan

A Pile of Stones, © 1998, CRC Publications, 2850 Kalamazoo Ave. SE, Grand Rapids, MI 49560. All rights reserved. No part of this book may be reproduced in any manner whatsoever without written permission from the publisher. Printed in the United States of America on recycled paper. ♻ 1-800-333-8300

Library of Congress Cataloging-in-Publication Data
Schut, Jessie, 1948-
    A pile of stones / by Jessie Schut.
      p.   cm.
    Summary: Seven children use primarily biblical stories and symbols to present forty devotions which express truths about the way God cares for His people.
    ISBN 1-56212-332-7
    1. Devotional calendars—Juvenile literature. 2. Children—Prayer books and devotions—English. 3. Bible stories, English. [1. Devotional calendars. 2. Prayer books and devotions. 3. Bible stories.] I. Title.
BV4870.S44   1998
242'.62—dc21   97-45747
                                                                   CIP
                                                               AC

10 9 8 7 6 5 4 3 2 1

Contents

Introduction 6

Tirzah
  1 The Beginning of the End of the Trip 8
  2 Walking Through the Water 10
  3 Dedicating a New Home 12
  4 I'm in the Army Now! 14

Clint
  5 The "Clint" Files (1) 18
  6 The "Clint" Files (2) 20
  7 The "Clint" Files (3) 22
  8 The "Clint" Files (4) 24

Deborah
  9 Waiting for War 28
  10 In Times of Trouble 30
  11 Passing on a Message of Hope 32
  12 Turning the Bad into Good 34

Arphaxad
  13 Grandpa Noah and the Beginning of the Story 38
  14 Messing Up God's World 40
  15 Obeying God's Voice 42
  16 Living with Rainbows 44

Mephibosheth
  17 Bad News 48
  18 When Life Fell Apart 50
  19 Called by the King 52
  20 Mephibosheth Remembers 54

Peter
  21 On the Outside, Looking In 58
  22 Amazing Doctor 60
  23 Awesome Teacher 62
  24 What a Friend! 64

Abigail

  25 News from Jerusalem 68

  26 Checking Out the Walls 70

  27 Work and Prayer: Weapons Against the Enemy 72

  28 Party Time! 74

Allie

  29 The First Day of School 78

  30 The Second Day of School 80

  31 The Third Day of School 82

  32 The Weekend 84

Reuben

  33 Reuben Keeps Watch 88

  34 Going the Distance for God 90

  35 Reuben in the Crowd 92

  36 Paul Preaches to the Crowd 94

  37 Reuben Visits Jail 96

  38 Reuben Overhears a Scary Secret 98

  39 Goodbye, Fear—Hello, Power 100

  40 A Letter from Caesarea 102

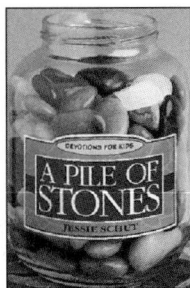

Dear Family,

As you read the stories in this book together, you might want to make your own "pile of stones." A good way to do that is to fill a large jar with flat stones and make it part of your devotional times together. Whenever members of the family are reminded of some way in which God has touched their lives, they could take a stone from the jar, draw a picture or write a few words about the event on it, and place it back in the jar. The illustrations found at the end of some of the stories in this book might serve as an inspiration and a good starting place for your own illustrations.

Periodically, you may want to empty the jar and "read" the stones together, remembering the wonderful things God has done. What a wonderful way to raise your own memorial to God's goodness!

Jessie Schut

Introduction

Because God is a Spirit, we can't see him, or touch him, or feel him. But humans are very sensory creatures—that's how God made us. So right from the very beginning, God revealed himself to his children through their senses. He spoke to Adam and Eve. He wrestled with Jacob. He told his people what kinds of furnishings to put in the temple and tabernacle. He gave visions and dreams to the prophets.

Jesus told stories people could identify with too, stories about farmers and housewives and shepherds. He gave his followers the Lord's Supper, with the symbols of bread and wine, to remind them of his broken body and shed blood. His followers baptized people to show them that their sins had been washed away.

In Deuteronomy, there's a fascinating passage in which God says, in effect, these words: "In the future, when your children ask about the meaning of your religious observances and practices, tell them a story about me—a story about how I have acted in the past, and how I will act in the future" (Deut. 6:20-25).

This book, *A Pile of Stones,* uses stories and symbols to tell the timeless truths of God. The stories are mostly Bible stories told from a child's point of view. I hope you and your family will be able to relate to the experiences, feelings, thoughts, and questions of the children in the stories so that the stories become real for you. Many of the stories contain a visual symbol that can help to remind you of some truth from God's story. For instance, the title *A Pile of Stones* comes from the memorial the Israelites created when they crossed the Jordan. The pile of stones symbol may not only remind you of the wonders God performed thousands of years ago, but also of the wonders God still performs in his children's lives today.

May this book of stories and symbols help you hear the story of how God extends his grace to all of us.

Jessie Schut

Tirzah

The Beginning of the End of the Trip

Read: Numbers 33:48-53; Joshua 2:1

Tirzah knew all about packing up and moving. Mount Hor, Zalmonah, Punon, Oboth . . . she'd lost track of all the places they'd been. And now, the order had come again: "Get ready. In three days we will go to the Jordan River. We're moving into the promised land."

Tirzah had felt shivers running up and down her spine. "This was it!" she had thought. Finally, the end of their trip was in sight.

Then Joshua had sent for her dad and their neighbor, Seth. Just before he had rushed off to see their leader, Tirzah's dad had said to her and her mom, "Start packing without me. I'll be back soon."

But now it was three nights later. Most everything was packed. Her mom was sound asleep, but Tirzah tossed on her mat. Her dad still wasn't back. Where was he? Tomorrow morning, when the order came to march, would they have to leave without him?

How on earth would they get across the Jordan River without drowning? And if they did get to the other side of the river, how would they defeat the enemy?

Tirzah crept to the door of the tent and sat there, looking out at the starry night. At daybreak, the adventure would begin. If only her dad would hurry home . . . Just then she saw a familiar figure moving through the shadows.

"Dad!" she whispered gladly. "Dad! You're back! Where were you?"

Her dad crouched down and hugged her. "Oh, Tirzah! I have seen such things—I've been across the Jordan into the promised land. Joshua asked Seth and me to check out the city of Jericho."

Tirzah stifled an excited squeal. "Tell me about it, quick!" she ordered.

"The people of Jericho are as jittery as jackrabbits. They fear the Israelites will conquer the land—so every stranger is an enemy," he whispered. "We could feel the suspicion all around us, so we ducked into an inn, and a kind woman named Rahab befriended us. She hid us under some straw on the roof of her house—and just in time. Some soldiers were there a few minutes later, asking about the strangers."

"Were you caught? Is that why you were away so long?" asked Tirzah anxiously.

"No, Rahab sent them on a wild goose chase, and then, in the night, she let us down out of her house on the wall on a rope," said Tirzah's dad. "She told us to hide in the hills until we could return here safely.

"When Jericho falls," he added, "God will save that brave woman and her family. She has acted wisely for God's sake."

His words reminded Tirzah about all her worries. "But Dad, how are we going to cross the river? How are we going to knock down the walls of the enemy cities? What will happen? Aren't you scared?"

"So many questions about the future, Tirzah . . . but why are you worried?" asked her father. "Should we disobey God and stay on this side of the river because we're scared? No! We will go into the land. Even those wicked people know how powerful our God is, and even they believe that we will conquer them.

"Come on, let's get some sleep," he said, putting his arm around her shoulders. "In an hour or two, the trumpet will sound and we'll be on our way. God has some great plans for us—just you watch and see."

Talk About It: What does trust mean? Can you trust God?

Prayer: *Dear Lord, I would like to know what is going to happen to me in the future. But I can't know that. There's only one thing I can be sure of: you have it all planned for me. Please help me to trust you.*
Amen.

Walking Through the Water

Read: Joshua 3:14-17

They had a quick breakfast of manna, and then it was time to go. It had taken a lot of time to pack up all of those thousands of tents, all the household goods, and all the animals and the babies. But they had done it.

The long snake of people moved across the desert to the Jordan River. In the green valley beside the river, they unpacked their tents once again and settled down to wait. One day, two days, three days. . . .

Tirzah was nervous. Her mom and dad were nervous. The neighbors were nervous. Even the animals were restless, pawing the ground and snorting, and shaking their heads, wild-eyed. The water in the river was high, touching the tops of the banks and flowing over in some places. How could they all cross?

Then suddenly, a messenger from Joshua stood among them. "Tomorrow we will move out," he said. "These are your orders from Joshua: When you see the priests carrying the ark of the covenant of the Lord, you must follow it. The priests will show you the way to go. Get ready for a miracle. Tomorrow, says Joshua, the Lord will do amazing things among you."

Now the air in the camp was charged with excitement, as the message was repeated over and over. Follow the ark. Get ready for a miracle! The Lord will do amazing things.

Tirzah's neighbors and parents clapped each other on the back as they gathered in a group to discuss the exciting news. "Get ready for a miracle—that's what Joshua says," said Seth. "Why didn't we think of that? Of course, God's coming through for us, just like he has done before."

"Remember the stories our parents told us about the plagues God sent to Egypt?" said Tirzah's mother. "Remember how God turned water into blood, and dust into gnats? Remember how he sent flies all over Egypt, but not into our homes? How could we forget?"

"My dad told me that when we came out of Egypt, God sent an angel ahead of us," added Joram, their neighbor. "The angel was in a pillar of fire. He showed us where to go. God's always been with us, and now he'll do it again."

Then everyone started sharing stories of what their parents had told them about God's miracles: water from a rock when they were thirsty . . . bitter water turned to sweet . . . a dead stick, covered with blossoms . . . quails from the sky when they were hungry.

"And of course, God parted the Red Sea and led us through on dry ground when Pharaoh and his army were chasing us," said Tirzah's dad.

Tirzah listened, her eyes wide. Was God going to do it again? Was he going to make a dry path through the river? Impossible, wasn't it . . . or was it? Did God still do miracles like that for people?

She thought about it as she washed out the manna pots with water from the Jordan River. Tomorrow she'd go out to gather manna while her parents packed up the tent once again, and then they'd be on their way, ready to see what amazing things God would do.

Think About It: Sometimes miracles are so close to us that we don't see them. What miracle is Tirzah missing? What miracles might you be missing, even though they're close to you?

Prayer: *Dear God, every day you do miracles, but sometimes we don't notice. Open our eyes to a miracle today. In Jesus' miraculous name, Amen.*

Dedicating a New Home

Read: Joshua 4:19-24

Tirzah was a grouch. Even her dad, sick with fever and resting against a rock, had noticed her short temper and long face.

"Tirzah," he'd said, "I think we need to talk. Tonight when the sun goes down, if I'm feeling better, you and I will take a walk."

Later, in the moonlight, Tirzah and her dad walked across the field outside the camp to a tower of rocks. They settled down at its base.

"Now, Tirzah, tell me what's bothering you," said Tirzah's dad. "Here we are, in the land God gave us, and you look like you swallowed a bug."

"Okay, so where's the milk and honey everybody was talking about?" burst out Tirzah. "This land doesn't look a lot different from where we were before. Are we in the right place?"

"Is there anything else that's bothering you?" asked her dad.

"Yeah, how come we're not fighting big exciting battles?" said Tirzah. "We're just waiting around here at Gilgal. You guys are in no shape to fight. You all got circumcised, and you're all lying in your tents feeling sick. It's no fun."

"Anything else, while we're at it?" asked her dad with a smile.

"Yeah . . . what's this thing called Passover?" Tirzah asked. "I thought God was going to whip the enemies, but instead we're just waiting around remembering Egypt. I want to see God get busy right now! Maybe he changed his mind. Maybe God stayed on the other side of the Jordan."

"Well, that's quite a list of worries," said her dad. He was quiet for a while, but then he took Tirzah gently by the shoulders and turned her around to face the rock pile. "How did this rock pile get here, Tirzah?" he asked.

"Each tribe took a stone from the Jordan River and brought it here, Dad," said Tirzah impatiently. "When we look at it, we remember what God did at the Jordan River, piling up all the water and letting us go across on dry land."

"Right," said her dad. "That was pretty impressive, wasn't it?"

"Yeah," answered Tirzah reluctantly.

"God led us here, Tirzah. This is definitely going to be our new home. And God's going to be doing a lot more of those kinds of wonders," said her dad. "But we have to make sure we're ready for it. That's what circumcision and the Passover feast are all about—a reminder that we're people who belong to God, and that we can trust God to care for us always."

"You're sure he didn't forsake us, Dad?"

"I'm as sure that God's still with us as I am that this pile of rocks is real," answered her dad with a smile.

Tirzah was happier as she and her dad got up and went back to the camp. Tomorrow they would celebrate the Passover. And then they'd be ready to face the enemy.

Think About It: What kinds of things do you worry about? How does God remind you that he's in control?

Prayer: *Dearest Lord, when I worry, I think maybe you're not with me anymore. Remind me, like you did with the pile of rocks at Gilgal, that you're still around and doing great things. Amen.*

I'm in the Army Now!

Read: Joshua 6:12-16

It was the strangest army ever. And Tirzah, a young girl with no helmet or sword, no shield or armor, was one of the soldiers, walking around the walls of Jericho. It was an army of ordinary people, and the army commander was God himself.

Today was the sixth day all the people had quietly walked around the city behind the armed guards, the priests with their rams' horns and the ark of the covenant. The golden ark gleamed in the piercing sunlight. Shuffle, shuffle, shuffle . . . hundreds of thousands of pairs of sandals shuffled in the dirt.

Tirzah looked up, up, up: the walls were high and thick and strong—so strong and thick, houses were built right on them. From one of them hung a long, red rope; as they passed it, her father whispered, "That's where Rahab lives—that's the window where she let us down by a rope. Tomorrow, when the walls come tumbling down, you'll meet her."

Except for the trumpet blasts, the only sounds coming from this unusual army were footsteps on dirt—a constant shuffle, shuffle, shuffle.

Mothers hushed their babies; fathers kept a stern eye on the children. They were obeying the orders of their commander, God himself, who had said, "Just be quiet until I tell you the time has come. Then you may shout and praise me, for you will see wonders."

The first day, only a few people inside Jericho had dared to peer over the wall, their faces pale and frightened. The second day, a few more people were visible. Day by day, as nothing happened, they grew bolder, laughing and talking to each other as they watched the strange procession.

They jeered and taunted: "Look! It's an army—an army of women and children and holy men! Scary stuff, isn't it? Tremble, Jericho! They're going to get us—ooooh, yeah."

They made fun of God, the holy one. "What's the matter, is your god trying to get up the courage to fight? Is he trying to figure out a way of climbing over our walls? Fat chance! Some god you've got there, packed up in a crate." Their scornful laughter and catcalls rang in Tirzah's ears.

Shuffle, shuffle, shuffle . . .

She wanted to yell up at them, "Stop it! Can't you see? We don't need to fight! The Lord God himself is going to win this battle for us. You've seen how he has defeated other kings, how he's brought us across the Jordan. He's the only high and great God. Rahab believed, and she will be saved. Why not you?"

But instead, she kept walking. It wouldn't do any good to tell them. They didn't want to listen.

Shuffle, shuffle, shuffle. The quiet army walked on, trusting in their leader. Tomorrow God would show his power.

Think About It: Have you ever had to wait a long time for God to act? How did you feel while you were waiting?

Prayer: *Dear God, it must have taken a lot of faith for the Israelites to have kept walking around the walls of Jericho, quietly trusting in you. Please help me have that kind of faith too. Amen.*

Clint

The "Clint" Files (1)

Read: Genesis 12:1-8

Diary Entry (June 15)

I used to think that the day I got chicken pox, which was the same day my cat died, was the worst day of my life. I thought nothing worse could happen to me. But I was wrong. I don't think I can feel much lower than this.

I'm writing this down because I can't talk to my friends. I can't tell Mitch, or Brent, or even Jason, because they're not here. They're all about a thousand miles away from this icky, rickety motel we're staying in tonight.

My troubles started last fall. Dad was told that his job at Amalgamated Electric was finished. There was no more work. Nothing. Zip. When he tried to find work at other places, he struck out everywhere.

It was a bad winter. My mom still had her job, but Dad spent his days reading want ads and making phone calls. After a while, he didn't do much of that either. We never had any money for anything. And Dad got more and more depressed.

Then, a month ago, we got a letter in the mail. It had a foreign stamp on it, and Dad smiled for the first time in a long time. "Hey, it's from Uncle Charlie up in Gold River," he said. A minute later, he started grinning from ear to ear. But he didn't say anything till Mom got home, and then they went for a long walk together to talk over what was in the letter. Allie (my kid sister) and I wondered what was up.

It didn't take long to find out. It turns out that my great-uncle Charlie, who is the black sheep of the family, has a farm way up in northern Alberta (that's in Canada, in case you're wondering). Uncle Charlie's getting old, and he invited my dad to come up and work for him. And that's why we're staying in this ratty motel in Canada on our way to Gold River. Two more days of traveling, and we'll be there—in the middle of nowhere.

I don't get it. Why did this happen to us? Why did Dad lose his job? Why do we have to move? Why do I have to leave my friends and my school and my neighborhood? I think the rest of my life is ruined.

I asked Dad all those questions and more before we left. He said, "Clint, I didn't want to lose my job. But sometimes, bad things happen. Now, I believe Uncle Charlie's job offer is an opportunity sent by God. You know how we prayed and prayed that I would get a job, and God sent us this. I know it'll be hard for you to leave your friends, but you'll find new friends in Gold River. Maybe the change will be a great adventure for you too."

Well, maybe it will. But I don't think so. I wonder why God answers prayers in ways that we don't like. I think I'll ask him about that in my prayers tonight.

Think About It: Is it okay to ask God questions like Clint is asking? Will God listen to your questions?

Prayer: *Dear Lord, sometimes I wonder why bad things happen to me. I'd like to learn more about you and how you work in my life. Please help me listen and learn. In Jesus' name, Amen.*

The "Clint" Files (2)

Read: Genesis 2:4-15

Date: Mon, 29 June 1997 19:43:22-0500 (MST)
From: slave#1clint <baker@freenet.noral.ca>
To: Jason <pqmagee@chiclink.us
Subject: Alberta, home of the moose

Hi, Jason—

Bet you didn't know the boonies would have e-mail. Neither did I. But we just found this computer yesterday when we were cleaning out Uncle Charlie's room. Some slick salesman probably talked him into buying it. At least something is working out right.

This place is something else.

For one thing, there's my great-uncle Charlie. Picture the Beverly Hillbillies' Jed Clampet, only half the size and twice as old. That's Uncle Charlie. He stayed around for a day or two after we got here, and then he left for Edmonton, a big city about four hours away. He has a doctor's appointment there.

And then there's the farm, which is kind of falling apart. Uncle Charlie hasn't been able to keep up with the work, so everything needs fixing—like the chicken coops, the fences, the barn door, the tractor, the well pump, the kitchen sink. At least the crops are planted—some neighbors helped Uncle Charlie with that this spring.

My mom just about died when she saw the house. It's going to take a million years to clean up Uncle Charlie's mess. And guess who's helping Mom do that? Allie and me, of course. All we do is work, trying to get the place in shape.

After supper tonight, we read from the Bible for devotions—all about Adam and Eve taking care of the Garden of Eden. Dad was pretty excited. He said, "That's what we're doing—we're tending the earth, taking care of it for God."

He doesn't see the mess—he's just thinking about what it will be like when it's all fixed up. He was telling us about what still needs to be done—stuff like mending fences, picking up rocks from the fields, etc. I wonder who gets to do that?

Mom let out a big sigh, Allie started bawling and saying she wanted to go back to Chicago, and I yelled at Dad, "Why do we have to work all the time?"

Dad looked real surprised. He scratched his head and was quiet for a minute.

"I'm sorry," he said. "I've been running you all pretty hard, haven't I? In a perfect world, taking care of this place would be pure joy. But this isn't a perfect world, or a perfect farm either. I think we need a break. So how 'bout we take the day off tomorrow to explore the countryside?"

Hey, I don't think there's much out there to see, but it's gotta be better than work. I'll write again tomorrow. Write back, okay?

Clint

Talk About It: Would people still have to work if Adam and Eve had not sinned? What would be different about work?

Prayer: *Dear Lord, you gave us a big world to take care of. Sometimes we get tired and cranky. Please forgive us and help us do the best we can. Amen.*

The "Clint" Files (3)

Read: John 11:1-3, 32-44

July 18

Dear Jeremy,

Hey, guy, where are you? I thought you said you'd write me every week. So far I have only gotten one letter from you. What's going on with you, anyway? You said in your letter you were tired, but how much energy does it take to write a friend a letter?

Everything here is okay, I guess. Not great, but okay. It's pretty boring without you guys around, though. I miss skateboarding, McDonald's, and seeing the latest copy of *Mad* magazine.

Write soon! Clint

* * * * * * *

Diary Entry, July 29

The hotter it gets, the more mosquitoes come out. It was very hot today. I never knew those little bloodsuckers could do so much damage to a guy.

Haven't heard from Jeremy, even though I sent him another letter. What's the matter with him, anyway? I knew the other guys wouldn't write, but I thought I could count on Jeremy.

* * * * * * *

Church bulletin, Living Waters Community Church, Chicago, July 24

Our Church Family: Please pray for the Bader family, especially Jeremy Bader. Last week he entered the hospital for tests to find out why he's tired all the time. More tests will be done this week.

* * * * * * *

Newspaper clipping sent in a letter from a friend of Clint's mom

Chicago

Living Waters Community Church members rolled up their sleeves Saturday morning and got to work.

Their job was to donate blood to help one of their members, twelve-year-old Jeremy Bader. Bader has a rare blood disease that requires regular transfusions of blood. His friends at church were quick to offer their help.

"We know Jeremy will need these transfusions often, and we wanted to help. We came up with this idea," said Pastor Ron Black. "We're the family of God together, and so Jeremy is our brother. The blood Jeremy can't use will be passed on to the hospital."

* * * * * * *

Get Well Card

Jeremy—

Hey, forget that nasty note I sent you about not writing. I'm sorry you're so sick.

You shouldn't be sick—you were always stronger than me. And your family was even into health food.

I told my mom God should pick on some criminal or a crook, not on a kid. She said, "God isn't picking on him. In fact, God is sad too. He's sad because sin ruined his perfect world, and it didn't have to be like this."

I'm not sure I understand, but at least I'm glad to know that God isn't picking on you. Get well soon.

Your friend, Clint

Think About It: God is sad when people get sick. What other things do you think make God sad?

Prayer: *Dear Lord, when you made the world, it was beautiful, and you said, "It is good." How do you feel about it now? It makes me sad that bad things happen. Jesus, come again soon, and make our world new again. In Jesus' loving name, Amen.*

The "Clint" Files (4)

Read: Psalm 23

September 7
Clint Baker

How I Spent My Summer Vacation

This is an essay about how I spent my summer vacation. Actually, my family didn't have a summer vacation because we were moving to this place, and when we got here we worked all summer.

I didn't want to move. I didn't think it was fair. I guess I still don't think it's fair, but some parts of it haven't been as bad as I thought they were going to be.

The best part of moving was meeting my great-uncle Charlie, whose farm we took over. His wife died about five years ago, and he was really lonely until we came. He thinks it's great that he has a family now.

The best thing about Uncle Charlie is that he can tell some pretty good stories. He likes to tell stories about when he was young. When he was a kid, he moved too, just like me. Uncle Charlie and his mom and dad came to Canada from Europe on a big ship. They didn't know anybody, and they couldn't speak English. I can't even imagine how weird that must have been.

Uncle Charlie said that, every day on their trip, he and his mom and dad would start the day by reading Psalm 23. It helped them remember that even though they were going through hard, strange times, God would see them through.

This is a true story Uncle Charlie told me:

"After we got off the boat, we had to take the train to Edmonton. It was a long, long trip. When we got to Edmonton, we moved into a boarding house.

"The next morning, my mom and dad started talking about school for me. I was so scared! I didn't want to go to a school where I couldn't speak the language.

"We heard kids' voices outside, and when we looked out the window of the boardinghouse, we saw children walking by. They were carrying schoolbags.

" 'Look, Charlie,' my dad said. 'They're on their way to school. You go to school too, and learn English. Then you can help your mom and me when we look for a job.'

"You know what he did? He said a quick morning prayer with me, gave me a hug, and shoved me out the door. He said, 'Follow those kids, Charlie, and they will take you to school.' He didn't even go with me. I had to go all by myself. It was the hardest thing I ever did."

Uncle Charlie told me that story last week, after I said I didn't want to go to school and that maybe I should stay home and work with my dad in the fields.

Uncle Charlie said, "Staying out in the fields isn't going to get you very far, Clint. Sometimes you need to walk through some valleys and shadows if you want to get somewhere."

This essay turned out to be more about Uncle Charlie than about my summer vacation. I guess the most important part of summer was figuring out that if God took care of Uncle Charlie during his move, he'll take care of me too.

Think About It: Have you been scared about new experiences? What helped you get through them?

Prayer: *Thanks, God, that you are with me, that you lead me beside quiet waters, and that I don't have to be afraid because you take care of me like a shepherd takes care of the sheep. Amen.*

Deborah

Waiting for War

Read: 1 Kings 20:1-3, 13-22

Deborah knew she should stay close to the house, but the temptation to find out what was happening was too strong. She decided to sneak to the edge of the village to see if there was any sign of the enemy.

"Be careful, Deborah," her father had said to her sternly that morning. "Stay close to the house, close to your mother. And if they should appear, you know what to do, don't you?"

"Yes, Father," Deborah had said meekly, bowing her head. "I must run with Mother to the cave in the cliff and hide there. I must be very quiet. And you will come to the cave too."

"Good girl," said her father approvingly. "Whatever you do, don't try to protect our house or our goods. You'll be no match for them."

"But Father," protested Deborah, "the Arameans have no right to come into our land and take our food and kidnap us. We have a peace treaty with them. We should fight for what's ours. It's not fair that we should run and hide."

"You're right, we do have a treaty with them," said her father patiently. "But we live close to the border here, and the Arameans think the border should be moved. So they send raiding parties to chase us out."

"But God gave us this land, Father! You said that yourself. So why isn't God chasing them away? They're followers of the Evil One. God should strike them dead!" exclaimed Deborah.

Her father smiled sadly. "Deborah, Deborah! Have you seen the altar to Baal in the high place in our town? Have you seen how people are bowing down to false idols and worshiping the foreign gods? God warned us that we must worship only him or war and famine would come to us, but many people have disobeyed his commands. God warned us that we would be punished, but we didn't listen. Now we are weak, because God's power is not in us. Our nation has forgotten God, and now the Arameans can easily defeat us."

Deborah thought about her father's words all morning as she helped her mother bake bread and sweep the floors of the house. Waiting to see if anything would happen was awful. She wanted to do something.

And so now she was crouched behind a bush, peering out over the valley below, watching for a sign that the enemy would strike their village. Heat waves shimmered and danced over the sunbaked earth, and even the crickets were silenced by the hot noonday sun. Would the raiders come on a day like today, or would they wait till nightfall, when darkness covered their sneaky movements into the town?

"Most Holy God," Deborah whispered prayerfully, "we don't deserve your protection, but we sure do need it. Please be with us."

Think About It: How did the Israelites disobey God's commands? What was the result? Have you ever done something you knew was wrong and gotten caught at it?

Prayer: *Lord God, you ask us to worship you, and you alone. Help us to push other things out of the way to make room for you. Amen.*

In Times of Trouble

Read: 2 Kings 5:1-2

The strange woman in the beautiful clothes made a babble of sounds that Deborah couldn't understand. The slave dealer said gruffly, "Deborah. Her name is Deborah."

"Dev . . . Devorah?" said the woman hesitantly. "Devorah!"

Deborah kept her eyes fixed on the tiled floor where she was kneeling. The woman gently lifted Deborah's bent head till their eyes were gazing into each other's. She nodded and smiled, and a servant who was with her handed a bag of coins to the slave dealer. He prodded Deborah, motioning for her to follow the woman.

Deborah awkwardly rose to her feet.

This nightmare she was in had started when she had slipped from her house to see if the raiders were coming. She hadn't heard the footsteps until it was too late—the crunch of sandals on gravel had come just a split second before big hands had grabbed her from behind and pulled her from her hiding place.

The raiding party struck quickly, and they left quickly too, taking along their captives and booty and leaving behind a ruined village, crops burning in the fields, and houses and barns empty. That's how she had come to be in this slave trader's market.

So many things had happened in the last week, and they had all been bad. Could something good come from it all? Would she never again see her mother and father, never again run through the fields and laugh with her friends? What could she do? Why had this happened to her? And what would happen now?

The questions tumbled through her mind as she lay on a mat in the servants' quarters later that night. Now she belonged to a man named Naaman; she would be the personal slave of his wife. Naaman worked in the Aramean king's army and was a very important man. She was living in the house of the enemy—all alone, far from home. Far from her father and mother, and far from her God, she thought.

Deborah thought about what her father had told her. He had said, "God warned us that this would happen, but we didn't listen. Now we are weak, because God's power is not in us. Our nation has forgotten God, and now the Arameans can easily defeat us."

Sometimes it's our own fault when bad things happen, she thought. The enemy caught me when I disobeyed my father, who had told me to stay home. If I had stayed home, Mom and I could have hidden in the cave, like Dad said, and I wouldn't be here now. She thought about how sad her father and mother must be feeling about what she had done.

She thought about other things her father and mother had taught her about God—that he had made her, and that he was everywhere.

"I'm sorry, God," she whispered in prayer. "My father said that if I do wrong and repent, you will forgive me. I am so sorry for disobeying my parents, and for disobeying you and making you sad."

Deborah realized that, even though her mom and dad weren't with her, she wasn't alone after all: someone was with her in enemy territory, and that someone would be with her whatever happened. Even when she was in big trouble.

Think About It: Is God with you wherever you go and whatever you do? Is he with you in times of trouble too?

Prayer: *God, I am glad you are every-where, even right here as I talk to you. You are great and awe-some and holy, but you are our friend too. Thank you. Amen.*

Passing on a Message of Hope

Read: 2 Kings 5:2-7

"Deborah!" The mistress was calling.

Deborah had been working for Naaman's wife for half a year. She could now speak and understand the language her mistress spoke. She hurried to the mistress and found her at the household shrine, burning incense to a god. Strange, how these people worshiped idols and tried to keep the gods happy with offerings and bribes.

Deborah bowed before her mistress, waiting for instructions. Her owners were kind to her. She lived in a beautiful house, and was well fed and clothed. Sometimes she almost forgot that she was a prisoner, that she was living with the enemy. Almost, but not quite.

The mistress looked worried and upset. "Deborah, what gods do your people pray to when they have a skin sickness? I have been burning incense here for months, begging the gods for help. But they are not listening! Naaman's sickness is becoming worse."

Deborah knew that Naaman, the master, was ill with the dreaded leprosy. In spite of his riches and his obedience to his gods, a bad thing was happening to Naaman, her good master. God's enemy Satan, who brought unhappiness to people, was at work here in this land too.

"Perhaps there's no hope anymore," moaned the mistress. "Oh, dear gods, what have we done wrong to be punished with this—this—horror?" And the mistress began to weep.

Was there really no hope for her master? How horrible it must be for him. Her master was a prisoner of his illness, and he didn't even have God to help him through it.

Deborah was a prisoner, too, but she was luckier than Naaman. She had hope. She knew that, with God, anything was possible. Every night she prayed to God that someday she would see her family again.

"Don't worry," urged Deborah. "There is hope! I know someone who can heal the master."

The mistress stared at Deborah. "Tell me, tell me quickly," she urged Deborah.

"The most high God, my God who made heaven and earth, he can heal Naaman. In my land, there is a prophet who will pray for Naaman. And God can heal him," said Deborah.

The mistress grabbed Deborah by the sleeve. "Come, come with me. We must tell Naaman. Maybe this god of yours will be gracious."

Now Naaman was leaving on a trip to *her* country. He was full of hope and excitement, expecting that this new god would do what his own gods could not. Deborah knew that God could heal Naaman, and she prayed that Naaman would not be disappointed.

She watched him ride away with his servants and chariots and horses, riding away with hope in his heart for healing. How she wished she could go! Perhaps some day . . . for the God who could heal Naaman could do great things in Deborah's life too—she was sure.

Think About It: Naaman put his hope in false gods when he had a problem. When you have a problem, do you sometimes put your hope in the wrong thing?

Prayer: *Dear God, when you sent your son Jesus to earth, you gave us hope for help in this life and forever and ever when we live with you in heaven. Thank you for knowing what we really need. Amen.*

Turning the Bad into Good

Read: 2 Kings 5:8-14

The master was back! The house was abuzz with excitement. The master was back, and he was healed! The dreaded skin disease was gone.

In the servants' quarters, the men who had gone with him told the whole story to the rest of the servants. Deborah sat in a corner and listened while the conversation went on.

The servants told about the visit to the foreign king who had been all confused and upset. He had finally sent them to a prophet, who had given them a message through his lowly servant: "Go wash in the Jordan River."

"Imagine," one of the servants said. "A servant ordering our noble master around like he was a peasant, telling him to wash in that mud hole. Naaman was so angry he just about turned around and went home."

"He was more than mad. He was embarrassed and ashamed," agreed another. "But we talked him into it. What's the harm in trying? we told him. It won't cost you anything. And it's not something hard he's asking of you. So finally, he did it: he went to the Jordan River, and dipped himself in seven times. When he came out the last time, his skin was as pink and healthy as a newborn baby's."

The listeners shook their heads in amazement. What a powerful God this must be, to be able to use muddy water and make someone clean again, one of them said. Another wondered at how ordinary it all seemed.

"It's a strange way for a god to act, don't you think?" he said. "It seems that he speaks through ordinary people—like you or me, even. No flashes of lightning, no bolts of thunder, no priests casting spells or sacrificing bulls. I've never heard of such a god before."

This was truly astonishing news. A God who could heal, but who didn't need sacrifices; a God who spoke through ordinary people, and would listen. The servants had never heard of such a God before. Perhaps they could worship this God too—but how?

"Naaman has brought back soil from Samaria," reported the servant. "On this soil, he is going to build a shrine so that he can make a place to worship the God who is more powerful than any other god. He says that now he knows there is no other god like this God."

Deborah sat in her quiet corner and listened and watched. She saw that the servants were puzzled and curious. They wanted to know more. Who would teach them? Wasn't there someone here who could tell them about this God who was like no other that they knew?

Deborah took a deep breath. Well, someday, she hoped, God would let her go home to her own people. But while she was here, it seemed as though he had some plans for her.

She opened her mouth and began to tell the others what she knew about this wonderful God of hers.

Think About It: Who is in control of your life? Can you trust God, even when bad things happen to you?

Prayer: *God, you are awesome! You have plans for my life that I do not understand, but help me to trust you whatever happens. I know you care for me, and I love you. Amen.*

Arphaxad

Grandpa Noah and the Beginning of the Story

Read: Genesis 5:1-2; 6:9

My name is Arphaxad.

Don't laugh! You've probably never met a person named Arphaxad, but it's a perfectly normal name where I come from. I live in Mesopotamia, a fertile valley that lies between two huge rivers.

Our family is a farming family. My grandfather, Noah, my dad, Shem, and my uncles, Ham and Japheth, work together to grow plants and raise animals. It's a good life.

My grandfather is a pretty old man—614 years old, would you believe? He was 603 years old when I was born, and my dad was 100. One of my ancestors, Methuselah, lived to be 969 years old. So I guess that means my grandpa is just a little past middle age.

My grandfather and I work together in the fields. My grandfather loves being outdoors, but I get kind of tired of it sometimes. On one particularly hot day, I started to complain, "This sun is killing me. I wish it would just go away for a while."

Usually Grandpa Noah is pretty easygoing, but that time he acted real upset. He grabbed me by the shoulders. "Don't ever say that again," he commanded. "The sun won't kill you, boy. Water does a better job of that. If you'd seen all that rain and water that I once saw, you'd never complain about sunshine again."

His eyes stared into mine. It was the look he got whenever someone talked about the days of the flood. Then he shuddered and turned away. My words had reminded Grandpa Noah of some pretty awful things—memories of a different time in his life.

I'd heard the stories before—the story of the big flood, and the boat, and the animals. I'd missed out on it all—I wasn't even born then. It sounded exciting to me, like being on a cruise. And every kind of animal was on that boat. Imagine, being able to pet a lion or ride on the back of an elephant. So why was Grandpa getting upset? I decided to find out.

When we got to the end of the row and were ready to take a rest in the shade of a bush, I took a deep breath and said, "Grandpa, how did it all start, anyway? The rain, I mean, and the floods? And why was it so awful? And how did you know that you had to build a boat? Tell me the story of the flood. I've heard people talking about it, but I want to know more."

Grandpa Noah nodded. "You're right, you need to know the story. We need to remember what happened, because the story isn't finished yet," he said. "It's the story of God and people; you and I, and our whole family, and anyone who has ever lived is part of it. It's a long story, but I guess we can get started now."

Grandpa and I put down our hoes, got settled in the shade, and he began: "Well, it all started with Adam and Eve, son. . . ."

Think About It: What did Adam and Eve do that changed the world? Why do we need to remember Adam and Eve and Noah?

Prayer: *Thank you for the stories you tell in the Bible that remind us of you. We learn how much you love us, and how often we do things that make you sad. And we learn about the promises you make to us, to always love us. Thanks for people who tell us about you. Amen.*

Messing Up God's World

Read: Genesis 6:4-14

"Yes, it all started with Adam and Eve, the grandparents of every-one who has ever lived," said Grandpa Noah. "When God created people, he made them perfect like himself.

"That was quite a wonderful time," said Grandpa. "Every day Adam and Eve worked in their beautiful garden home, and every evening God came down to visit with them. I wish I could have been there."

I tried to imagine what it must have been like, talking and visiting with God. He would have been right there with them, not far away.

"And then our first ancestors sinned," Grandpa continued. "Adam and Eve broke the beautiful relationship they had with God. And now all of us are like Adam and Eve—kind of scared of God, wishing we could be close to him again, but not sure how to do it."

"But Grandpa, what does that have to do with the flood? Adam and Eve lived many, many generations ago, but the flood happened only twelve years ago," I said.

"Adam and Eve's sin started it," said Grandpa Noah. "After that, people started to drift away from God, and they chose wicked people to be their friends and heroes. People stopped asking, 'What does God want us to do?' and started asking, 'What do I want to do?'"

"Is that how it was when you were young, Grandpa?" I asked.

Grandpa's face was sorrowful. There were tears in his eyes. "When I was young, Arphaxad, it was a horrible time. People scoffed and mocked at the idea of a God who made them. If they were angry, they killed and robbed and mistreated each other. If they felt good, they praised themselves. They thought of themselves as gods, and they worshiped themselves."

"I wonder how God felt when that happened, Grandpa," I said. "He made people to be his friends, and then they turned their backs on him. Did he get mad?"

I was getting kind of mad myself. That sure wasn't fair to God—they should have treated him better.

Grandpa Noah shook his head. "God felt the way you would if something beautiful and precious that you owned got messed up. He cried. He felt sad and sorrowful. He was sorry that he had ever made this world. That's how God felt, Arphaxad. And that's still how he feels when we mess up.

"But listen, we need to get back to work. I'll finish telling you the story of the flood after supper. That way, your brothers and your cousins can hear it as well. We should never forget the stories about God's deeds in this world."

Think About It: The Nephilim—people of great size and strength—were the "heroes of old" (v. 4). Who are your heroes? Do your heroes help you grow closer to God, or do they tempt you to disobey?

Prayer: *Lord, I'm sorry that your beautiful world got messed up. Thank you for your son Jesus, who came to fix it up again. Please help me to be your partner in making my home, my school, my community, and this world a better place. Amen.*

Obeying God's Voice

Read: Genesis 7:1-12

After supper that evening, Grandpa started right in with his story. My brothers and sisters and cousins were gathered around him in the tent.

"Actually, in this region, with rivers on either side of us, flooding happens quite often," said Grandpa. "But when God spoke to me, he warned me of a flood that would be like no other. It would wipe away everything around us—our farms, our animals, our crops, our tools, and our neighbors."

We were all perfectly silent in the tent as we tried to imagine what a scary message that must have been. Except for my big brother Asshur, that is. He was dropping little pebbles down the back of my tunic. I gave him an elbow to let him know I didn't think he was funny. I wanted to hear Grandpa's story.

"It scared me to think of such a thing," continued Grandpa. "But God is God: he does not lie. Maybe he tried to tell my wicked neighbors the same thing. But if they didn't believe in God, they couldn't very well believe his message, could they? Later, I tried to tell them, but they wouldn't believe me either."

Asshur wasn't listening to *my* messages, either. I was sending dirty looks his way, telling him to lay off, but as soon as I turned my back to him I felt another pebble sliding down my back. This one had a sharp edge that scratched as it went down. I was beginning to get mad.

"God told me what to do to save my family," Grandpa continued. "I had to build a huge boat—big enough to hold the family, as well as hundreds of different kinds of animals, and food for us all. It was a huge job—even with your dads helping it took 120 years."

"Did you ever think about quitting, Grandpa?" asked my little brother, Lud.

"I wanted to quit sometimes. It wasn't easy, especially when people teased us for building a boat in the middle of dry land, and for believing a message from a God they thought was a fairy tale," said Grandpa.

It sounded to me like the way Asshur teases me. Sometimes siblings are a pain. Maybe if I had some friends to play with it would be different, but after the flood, we were the only folks left.

Those pebbles down my back were really getting to me. When I saw my chance, I bopped him a good one, but he hit me right back. I was so mad, I couldn't think straight anymore. I was so sick of him! I jumped on him, pounding him out.

Suddenly, it was all over: my dad was hanging on to Asshur, and Grandpa had me by the collar. We kicked and hollered a little more, but it wasn't much use.

"He started it!" I yelled. But Asshur was wiping the blood off his nose and pointing the finger at me. "I did not," he howled. "You did."

Grandpa looked at my dad and shook his head. "Things haven't changed a lot since the flood, have they?"

Well, that got me thinking. The earth was destroyed in the flood, but sin is still around. Asshur and I proved that. I wondered what it would take to get rid of sin, finally and forever.

I'm glad God isn't finished with this world yet. I'm glad he's still telling the story. I hope it has a happy ending.

Think About It: Can you get rid of sin in your life, finally and forever? How can that be done?

Prayer: *Lord God, sin doesn't get washed away by a flood. It doesn't get excused away by smooth talking. It doesn't disappear if I ignore it. Sin stays in my life until I confess it to you and you forgive me for Jesus' sake. And then, Lord, you forget that it even existed. Thanks for your forgiveness, God. Help me to serve you by getting rid of the sin in my life. Amen.*

Living with Rainbows

Read: Genesis 9:8-16

After Asshur and I had made up (sort of) under Grandpa's eagle eye, we got settled to listen to the rest of the story. This time, I sat far away from Asshur.

"Well, we worked on that boat for a long, long time," continued Grandpa. "But when the work was finally done, I couldn't be happy. I knew what was going to happen."

"And then the flood came, and you ran into the boat. Isn't that right, Grandpa?" asked Lud.

"Actually, it happened the other way around, Lud," explained Grandpa. "One bright and sunshiny day, God said to me, 'It's time, Noah. Take your family into the ark.' And we did, even though there wasn't a drop of rain in sight.

"Then the animals began to come—tiny hummingbirds and enormous elephants, chattering monkeys and braying donkeys, growling bears and lovable raccoons. Our heavenly Father was taking care of them, just like he was taking care of us."

"Wow!" said Lud. "I wish I had been there."

"It took seven days to load up the ark. The sun kept shining, and the neighbors kept fighting each other and mocking us." Grandpa's voice trailed off, and he was silent for a minute.

Then he went on. "When we were all on board, God's hand closed the door. That's when it began to rain—forty days and nights of rain. It was the darkest time in our lives."

We were all imagining being in that boat, with rain and thunder and lightning all around. God's hand had closed the door, and only those who believed had been saved from the flood.

"I began to feel anxious," said Grandpa. "For months, we didn't see anything but water. I wondered if God had gone away and forgotten all about us, and if he would ever let us get off that boat again.

I really doubted that we would be able to live well enough to please God."

I shivered with worry. It was true: we seemed to be able to sin pretty quickly and easily. Would God come back and send another flood?

"What a relief it was for us when God said we could come back out and start a new life," said Grandpa. "The first thing I did was build an altar to praise and thank him for the wonderful way he had taken care of us."

"It was a new start for everyone. Only, the question was, could we please God, or would we mess up so badly that God would send another flood?"

He looked straight at me as he finished his story.

"Praise be to God, he answered that question right away. He said he would never again send such a horrible flood," said Grandpa. "He knew we might forget words, so he sent a beautiful symbol of his promise: a rainbow in the sky."

Grandpa gave me a hug as he finished his story. It felt good, like the feeling you get when you look at the rainbow. In fact, the rainbow is like a great big hug from God, promising us that he loves us. At least that's what I think.

Think About It: God's rainbow is a symbol of hope. So is the cross. What hope does the cross give to you?

Prayer: *Dear God, thank you for promises you make to us. You said that you would always be with us, and that, if we called to you, you would answer. Thank you for the rainbows, and cross-es, and bread and wine that remind us of your promises. Amen.*

Mephibosheth

Bad
News

Read: 1 Samuel 20:12-17; 28:4-6

Something bad was happening—Mephibosheth was sure of it.

But every time he asked his nanny what was going on, she just smiled nervously at him. "Why do you think something bad is happening?" she asked, stroking his fine hair.

"My mother looks worried, and she cries," said Mephibosheth. "Why is she crying? And where is my father? When will he come home?"

"I think your mother misses your father. He's been gone to war a long time," Nanny said.

Mephibosheth knew there was more to it than that. He hated it when grown-ups kept secrets from him. He knew that being a king, or a prince, was a dangerous job. Grandfather Saul had said so, and Grandfather was the king. He should know.

Mephibosheth stamped his foot. "I am a prince. You must respect me. Tell me what is happening to my father and to my grandfather. Why is everyone walking around with big worried looks? Why will nobody answer me when I ask questions? I order you to tell me, nanny!"

Nanny hid a little smile behind her hand. Mephibosheth seemed to have inherited his grandfather's temper—and his father's courage too. Even though he was only five years old, he certainly acted much older. How should she answer the prince?

The king and his three sons had left several weeks ago, calling the army together to fight again against the Philistines. Those godless enemies kept trying to wipe out the Israelites. And this time, she had heard rumors that thousands and thousands of their enemies were gathered to fight against Israel. What would happen to the household if the Israelites lost the battle?

Nanny knew that yesterday a messenger had come with bad news from the front lines. "Preparations are underway for the battle," he reported. "The king cannot sleep, and he walks about trembling with fright. The troops, too, are disheartened. They haven't had a word from the Lord to give them hope, and they are not sure they can win." That was why Mephibosheth's mother was frightened.

"It's true that we are worried," Nanny said, finally. "The news from the battlefront is not good. We must pray to Jehovah for protection."

Mephibosheth listened to her and was no longer angry. Now he was frightened. Sometimes, kings and princes died in battle. He wondered what he could do to help his father. Money wouldn't win a battle, and neither would crying and worrying. He could think of only one way to help his father, and that was to do as Nanny had suggested.

Mephibosheth tugged at his nanny's sleeve. "Come on, let's go and ask the priest to pray with us," he said.

And so Mephibosheth and his nanny went to ask the Lord for protection for the king and his sons and all the Israelites.

Think About It: Is there anything you shouldn't ask the Lord to help you with? Anything at all?

Prayer: *Lord God, sometimes very frightening things can happen, and I just don't know what to do. But I want to thank you that you will listen to us and comfort us when we are scared. In Jesus' name, Amen.*

When Life Fell Apart

Read: 1 Samuel 31:1-2; 2 Samuel 4:4

It was the middle of the night. All through the king's compound, the servants and family slept restlessly, their dreams filled with fearful images of battle.

Mephibosheth sat up. Something had awakened him. "Nanny, I hear something. What is it?" he asked.

An eerie, high-pitched wail, not loud but steady, drifted in through the open window.

Nanny sat up, too, straining to listen. The sound was swelling, growing louder. A crowd of weeping, moaning people were approaching the king's compound, and that could mean only one thing.

"Bad news from the battlefront," she whispered, jumping to her feet. "We have lost the battle. We must run to safety. There is no time to waste."

Mephibosheth watched Nanny scurrying about. He wanted to help, but his legs felt rooted to the ground. "Nanny," he cried. "I'm scared. Why do we have to run away? Why can't we stay here?"

Nanny gave Mephibosheth a quick hug and said, "I'm scared too, and I'd like to stay here, but we can't. Israel has lost the battle against the Philistines, Mephibosheth, and we don't know what's happened to your grandfather or your father. Before your father went to battle, he told us, 'If we lose the battle, you must take the family away until the turmoil is over. Take them to Lo Debar, to the house of Makir my friend. You will be safe there.'"

Mephibosheth remembered how his dad had talked to him too, before the battle. He had said, "You must be brave, son. Every time I go to battle, there's a chance that I will die. I know that God has chosen David to become king after my father Saul dies. So if we lose this battle, you must not be afraid, for David has promised that he will not harm you."

Now the time had come for Jonathan's family to run to safety. The quietness of the night had been changed to hustling and bustling. The courtyard was filled with servants rushing about, family members strapping on their sandals, and slaves loading up donkeys with household goods. And over it all was the sound of weeping and wailing at the tragedy that had happened.

Nanny knelt before Mephibosheth. "Are you okay?" she asked. Mephibosheth nodded.

"There's one thing you have to remember," she said as she boosted Mephibosheth up onto her back. "So much is happening, and we don't know how it will end. There's only one thing I'm sure of, though. Our God knows why this is happening. He is in control. Your father believed that too."

Nanny stood up with Mephibosheth clinging to her. "Hang on tight," she said. "We can go faster if I carry you. Come on, let's get moving."

Into the night they went—Nanny, Mephibosheth, and the others. And God went with them.

Think About It: What gave Jonathan courage when he went into battle? What can you count on when things don't go well?

Prayer: *Dear Lord, when I'm scared, could you please remind me that you are in control and that you know about my fears? Please comfort me with your love and care. Amen.*

Called by the King

Read: 2 Samuel 9:1-5

It was early morning at the house of Makir. Mephibosheth, sitting outside the tent, watched the hustle and bustle going on around him. Makir's household would be working hard today in the harvest. The servants were cooking food for the men to take to the fields.

When the men went to work, the camp became quiet. Only the women and the children and the household servants were left behind. And Mephibosheth.

"I should be out there, helping them," he thought for the hundredth time. "I wish I could be with the other men. I'm not a little kid anymore—boys of twelve are almost grown, ready to take their place alongside the men. Instead, I sit here."

Mephibosheth looked down at his legs. They looked like dried-out sticks, white and skinny. That's the way they'd been since that horrible night when his family had run to safety. He would never forget that long and awful night, clinging to his nanny, stumbling through the dark.

And then Nanny had tripped over a rock in the darkness, and he had been thrown through the air, landing with a crash on his head.

By the time they got to Makir's house, many days later, Mephibosheth couldn't feel a thing in his legs. Now he had been living at Makir's house for seven years, spending time watching others. Once he'd been a royal prince. Now he was a poor guest at Makir's house.

Mephibosheth picked up the flute he was whittling as he watched the men set off for the fields. Now there would be another boring day to get through. Perhaps, he thought, as he looked up to the horizon, someone might come to visit. That would make things a little more interesting.

In fact, someone *was* coming—perhaps a traveling caravan of merchants, by the looks of the dust cloud coming closer. But when the caravan approached Makir's house, Mephibosheth could see horses, and chariots, and pennants flapping briskly in the air. These weren't merchants, after all, but important visitors from the royal court of David.

Mephibosheth's heart began to race. What could it mean? Was Israel's new king hunting for the last of Saul's family so that he could kill him? "Jehovah God, I beg you, protect me from my enemies," he prayed silently.

Makir came out of the house and bowed low before the king's messengers. "Your humble servant offers hospitality," he said. "Come, and rest in our home."

But the servant shook his head impatiently. "We are looking for Mephibosheth, the son of Jonathan, the grandson of King Saul. Where is he?" Then, seeing Makir's agonized face, he hastened to add, "We mean the boy no harm. Our master, King David, wishes to show him kindness for his father's sake. He asks that Mephibosheth come to Jerusalem to live in the king's palace. We come to offer him a home and a refuge with the king."

Mephibosheth covered his mouth with his hand to hide the gasp of astonishment. An hour before, he had been feeling sad because his life was so boring. Just a moment before, he had been so frightened that he had begged God to protect him from his enemies. Now, it seemed, his worries and troubles had become blessings.

Once he'd been a royal prince. Then he'd become a poor guest. Now he'd be a royal prince once more. God was indeed gracious.

Think About It: What unexpected gifts has God given you today?

Prayer: *Dear Father, thank you for good gifts. Thank you for bringing unexpected blessings into my life. Please remind me of your love when I feel down and lonely and left out. Amen.*

Mephibosheth Remembers

Read: 2 Samuel 19:24-30

Jerusalem's citizens were rejoicing in the streets, dancing with happiness. "The war is over, and the king is coming back!" they shouted to each other.

In the palace, Mephibosheth heard the happy noises in the street and rejoiced. "Mica!" he shouted, "Mica, come quickly. Listen!"

Mica hurried to his father's side.

"Listen, son!" said Mephibosheth. "The king's men have defeated Absalom. King David is coming back to Jerusalem! Please help me saddle a donkey and ride to meet the king. I must welcome him home."

Mica nodded and smiled in relief. For weeks his father had stayed in a quiet corner of the palace, hardly eating or drinking, not combing his hair, not even bathing. Mephibosheth had been terribly sad because King David had been chased out of the city by his own son, who wanted to be the king. Now Mephibosheth was smiling again.

Soon they were riding on the road to meet the returning king.

"I wanted to go with David when he ran away," said Mephibosheth. "I told my servant Ziba to hurry and get my donkey ready. Even though I am lame, I wanted to be with my lord, King David."

"But you didn't go," said Mica. "Why not?"

"Ziba tricked me. He left me in Jerusalem while he took off," said Mephibosheth, sadly. "He's got a grudge against me. When I was living at Makir's house, Ziba took over all of my father's lands. When King David called me back to the palace, Ziba had to give the land back to me and become my servant. That must have been hard."

"But I saw Ziba loading the donkeys with food for the king," said Mica, puzzled.

"That's right. When David was hiding from his son Absalom, Ziba took him many gifts of food," said Mephibosheth. "It was my food he took to the king, but he told the king it was a gift from him. And he told the king, 'Mephibosheth doesn't want to be with you. He is waiting in Jerusalem, hoping to get the throne back when you are defeated.' King David believed Ziba, and gave him back the land that was mine."

"But that was a lie!" said Mica, angrily. "Ziba cheated us, and now we have nothing."

"Oh yes, it was a lie, and someday Ziba will have to answer to God for that," said Mephibosheth. "But Mica, don't say we have nothing. King David could have killed me, but instead he was gracious. He took me into his own home, fed me at his own table, and has always taken care of me. He showed me the kindness of God. So don't say we have nothing."

"Yes, Father," said Mica, meekly.

"Remember my story, Mica. I have had bad times in my life, but I have learned something very important. Even when I have nothing, I still have God with me, and that is everything I need. Everything!" exclaimed Mephibosheth, and he rode on to see the king.

Think About It: Do you find it hard to forgive people who do wrong to you? Are there such people now whom you need to forgive? Do it!

Prayer: *Lord, help me forgive others in the same way that you forgive me. That's a big order, Lord, and it's hard to do. So please bless me as I try to do your will. I love you, Lord. Amen.*

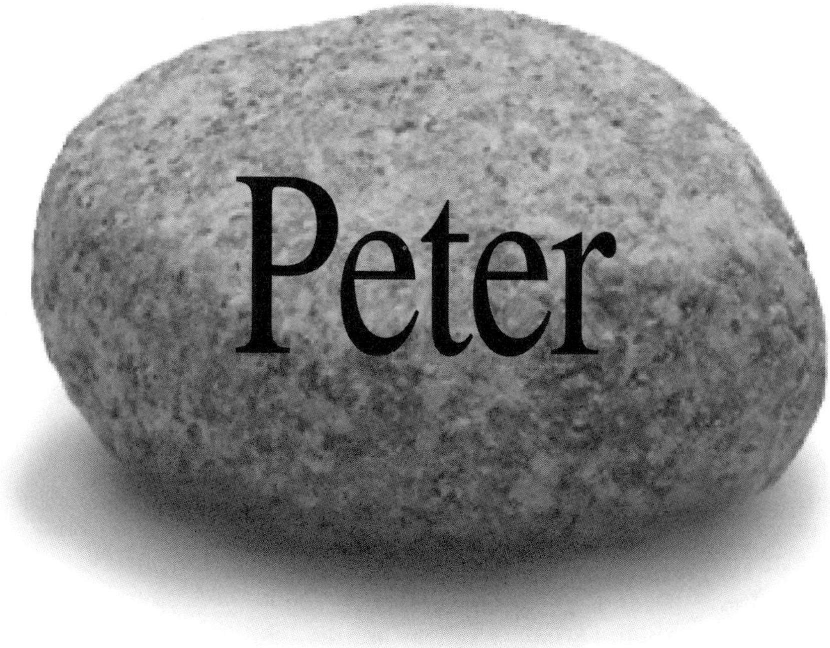
Peter

On the Outside, Looking In

Read: Mark 1:29-34

My name is Peter, and I need to tell you about the most important day in my life.

We were playing games, a bunch of us, and of course I was losing, when our moms, all excited, told us to get ready. We were going downtown to see a teacher called Jesus.

"People say he may be the Messiah," said my mom. "You never know—maybe he is. Here's our chance to see him."

It was a relief to quit the game. I think I was probably a loser from the time I was a baby. My mom says I was a "late bloomer." What she really means is that I was slower to walk and talk than every other kid around. I wouldn't know, 'cause I don't remember.

I do know that what other kids like James and Matthew do so easily takes me forever to learn. When the rabbi tells us to memorize parts of the Torah, I groan. All those words, all those complicated writings with the "thees" and "thous" and "thithers" make my head ache. They fly out of my brain as quickly as I try to stuff them in. I must have a hole in the back of my head.

My rabbi says that I have to try harder—that I'm just lazy. My dad gets worried when the rabbi says that, and then I feel worse than ever. And my mom is always making excuses for my problems. "Peter is so sensitive, he lies awake at night and worries," she tells her friends. "Then he's too tired to concentrate at school." Yeah, right.

The truth of the matter is that I'm just no good at things. Not even marbles. I wish I could be living out in the fields as a shepherd, looking after the sheep. Then I wouldn't have to go to school and learn things that don't make sense to me. I would love to look after the sheep. I think I might even be good at that.

I've heard about Jesus—people say he's smart and talented. He can argue with the Pharisees and rabbis, and he's better than the best doctor at healing sick people. So many people want to be his friend. He can have his pick. So it might be interesting to see him.

And maybe he is the Messiah, the one promised by the prophets to come and save his people. Maybe when I'm a grown-up. I'll be able to say, "I saw the Messiah when I was a kid. I saw him perform miracles."

But the thing that worries me is that Jesus might notice me. And then what will he say? He might say, "Why are you wasting my time?" Or he might pat me on the head with a pitying smile. Or he might ask me questions from the Torah, and I won't be able to answer.

I'm not sure I really want him to notice me. If he did, he'd probably be disappointed in me, like everybody else is. Let's face it—I'm not good enough.

Yes, we're going to see Jesus. I'll go along with my mom. But I'll keep out of sight so I won't have to meet him.

An important person like the Messiah . . . why would he want to meet me?

Think About It: Have you ever felt "not good enough," like Peter? Do you think Jesus will love you less if you're not good in some things, like sports or schoolwork?

Pray: *Lord, you had all kinds of friends. And you said I could be your friend too. I'm not sure why you'd do that, Jesus, but thank you. I'll accept your offer. From your friend, Amen.*

Amazing Doctor

Read: Matthew 19:1-2

I had never been in a crowd like this one. Just imagine a whole hospital emptying out, with all the patients out on the streets, and you'll get an idea of what it was like.

A man hobbling on sticks, dragging his useless feet behind him. A kid my age, whose eyes were blank and staring, being guided by his mom. And dozens more like them, sick, moaning, desperate. They were all coming to see Jesus.

I'd seen them around town before, begging for their living. They thought Jesus might be able to help them. But would he?

I remembered what our rabbi had said. "If you obey the laws, and do what God commands, you will be blessed. And if you don't, you will be cursed," he told us. That was sort of like saying that these people were sick because they'd sinned.

And if they were bad sinners, wouldn't Jesus know about it and tell them to go away? I saw the Pharisees and the teachers of the law gathered at the edge of the crowd, watching to see what Jesus would do. If Jesus said "Get out of here" to the sick people, then he'd pass their test; if he touched the sick, then he'd be a loser.

Suddenly the crowd parted. A man who had seen Jesus was coming back through. He was waving his crutches and shouting, "Look at me! I can walk! Praise God, I can walk!" His face was radiant with joy. "Jesus did it!" he exclaimed. "Doctors told me there was no hope—but this rabbi healed me. Truly, he is a man sent from God."

More people were returning from their visit with Jesus. These people who had been touched by Jesus were shouting and laughing and singing and jumping. They were full of joy! The sick people saw their healed friends, and they got pretty excited. "Let me through! I have to see Jesus!" shouted the mother of the blind boy.

The Pharisees stood and watched, arms folded across their chests, shaking their heads in disgust.

Hey! I don't get it. If Jesus is so powerful, how come he's taking valuable time to meet with all these nobodies? Why doesn't he treat them like the sinners they are?

If he's really and truly the Messiah, doesn't he have more important things to do, like getting rid of the evil Romans who are ruling our country? Would Jesus really rather spend time with sinners, with sick and crippled people? Does he think they're just as important as hotshots like Herod and Pilate? Why?

I just had another thought, a scary one. If Jesus thinks it's important to be with people who are nobodies, might he also feel the same way about talking to me and my friends? Could it be that, even though I'm not too eager to meet Jesus, he might be looking forward to visiting with me?

Impossible! Or is it?

Think About It: Is it possible that Jesus likes to spend time with children? How can you spend time with Jesus?

Prayer: *Lord Jesus, sometimes I forget that you are my friend, and I don't spend enough time with you. Please forgive me. Help me to remember to spend time with you, my best friend. Amen.*

Awesome Teacher

Read: Mark 10:1-2

We waited in the crowd for hours, watching. People "oohed" and "ahhed" as, one by one, the desperately sick were healed and ran off to share their good news with family and friends.

Finally, there were no sick folks left. Now Jesus seated himself on the hillside so people could see and hear his teachings. He didn't look all that special—no royal robes or crown, no special tunic like the teachers wear, just an ordinary man. If we'd passed him on the street, we wouldn't even have known he had such power.

The Pharisees had a whole long list of questions—like a test or something. "What do you think of divorce, Jesus?" they asked. And "Isn't it true that the Sabbath is a day of rest? Is it lawful to heal on such a day?" And "Do you obey our laws that say that you should always wash your hands before you eat?" And other questions like that.

Jesus patiently answered them, but it was boring stuff for kids. Is this why our moms had brought us to see Jesus? I really hadn't wanted to come at first, but now I had some questions of my own that needed answering—like "How did you do those healings? Can you turn stones into bread, so you never have to buy food? Who are you anyway?"

I guess that last one would have been the most important question. Who was Jesus? Was he really the Messiah, the one who had come from God to save his people? And did he really care about ordinary people like us who couldn't do anything right? That would be awesome!

While we sat and waited and waited and waited, our moms were getting restless. They really needed to go home and start cooking supper.

My mom finally sidled up to one of the disciples. "Sir," she said as she tugged at his sleeve. "Our children want to see Jesus. Can you help us get through to him?"

He laughed. "Did you hear that?" he asked the other disciples. "These women think Jesus has nothing more important to do than talk to kids!" He turned to my mother and said, "Jesus doesn't have time for your kids. Can't you see how busy he is? Go home!"

That's when I got mad! I needed to talk to Jesus. It was important. And these guys were going to send us away. I got an idea.

"Hey, Jesus!" I yelled as loud as I could. "Please, Jesus! Can I ask you some questions too? Please?"

Jesus raised his eyes and looked straight at me. I held my breath. What would he do?

Then he smiled! Jesus smiled at me, and he beckoned for us to come. I could hardly believe it, but Jesus wanted to visit with us.

What a healer! What a teacher! And what a friend!

Think About It: If Jesus came to your town, what questions would you ask him?

Prayer: *Dear Jesus, I have lots of questions, because there are things I don't understand. It's a good thing you know all the answers. Please help me trust you when things don't make sense. Amen.*

What a Friend!

Read: Mark 10:13-16

You should have seen those Pharisees' faces! When they realized Jesus wasn't going to answer anymore of their questions, they were furious.

The disciples weren't too pleased either. They thought they were doing Jesus a favor by keeping us away, and there he went and invited us to come to him.

But we were pretty excited. We pushed through the crowd and, suddenly, there we were, right in front of him—me, and my friends, and our moms in the background watching proudly.

"So you have some questions too?" he said with a smile, as he picked up a baby and set her on his knee. "I'm listening, so go ahead and ask."

I felt suddenly as though someone had tied a big knot in my tongue. This was my big chance, and I was blowing it.

Jesus grinned at me, as though he knew what was happening. He turned to the crowd.

"Look at these kids," he said. "Just look at them." The baby made a grab for Jesus' hair. "These kids are very, very important people."

The Pharisees and teachers began grumbling to each other. "Is he saying these little squirts are more important than we are? Ridiculous! We are the guardians of the kingdom of God."

"These kids wanted to come and see me, to ask me questions," Jesus said to his disciples. "You wanted to stop them. Don't do that!" Now his voice was stern. "The kingdom of God belongs to children like this."

Whoa! Was he talking about us? The kingdom of God belonged to us? To me, with my tied tongue and my wanting to run away and hide? Whaaaat?

"This boy here," he said, touching my shoulder, "wanted to ask me a question. His questions are just as important as anybody's. So listen to him and to the children."

The crowd was really quiet now. Jesus' eyes looked into mine. He really wanted to know what I was thinking! He didn't think I was stupid at all.

Well, those Pharisees and teachers could argue all day about the laws and the Sabbath and stuff like that. I had more important things to do. I gulped a deep breath.

"I want to know all about you," I said, and then, before I lost my nerve, added, "You're awesome. I want to be your friend. Can I follow you?" And he nodded gladly and hugged me.

I think I've found something I can do now. I don't feel so dumb after all.

Like I said at the beginning of my story, the day I met Jesus and became his follower was the most important day in my life. I hope you meet Jesus too.

Think About It: Have you met Jesus? Is he your friend too?

Prayer: *Jesus, I want to follow you. Please teach me all about you and your kingdom. And thank you for saying that kids are important. That's good to know. Amen.*

Abigail

News from Jerusalem

Read: Psalm 137:1-6

Living in the luxurious palace of King Artaxerxes here in Babylon is a pretty good deal. I get to eat and drink at the king's table, wear fancy clothes, and never have to worry.

My name is Abigail, and my dad, whose name is Nehemiah, is the cupbearer to the king. The king trusts my father, so we have a good life. Sometimes it's easy to forget that we're foreigners and that we really don't belong here.

Sometimes *I* may forget that I'm a foreigner, but my dad never does. Whenever he catches me acting like a Babylonian, he sits me down and tells me the story I've heard so many times before. "We are God's chosen people," he says. "He led us to the promised land, where we had a good life. But we turned to other gods and wouldn't listen to the prophets, so God finally let the Babylonians come and take us away."

"Abigail, this is not our home," he keeps saying. "Some of our people have already gone back to Jerusalem to rebuild God's temple. Ezra the priest is leading the people in repairing the city. God is gracious. Maybe soon we too will go back to our own country, to the land God gave us."

But I'm wondering . . . who wants to go to a broken-down city in a far-off land when they could have all this luxury? Really, we can worship God anyplace, can't we? I don't understand why my father is so passionate about it.

But now I find out I don't have a choice. We're going back, and my father is going to lead the way. This is how it happened.

My uncle Hanani, who was working for the king in Jerusalem, came back for a visit in the fall. The first thing my dad asked him was, "Tell me about Jerusalem. Has Ezra the priest succeeded in rebuilding the city?"

Uncle Hanani told him the truth. "It's a mess, Nehemiah. The walls around the city are torn down, and the gates are burned. Our enemies—their names are Sanballat and Tobiah—have harassed us so badly, the work has stopped. Everyone is discouraged and wonders why they've come back."

My father got really upset. He spent hours in the prayer closet every day, and sometimes I could hear him crying in there. It got so he had a hard time eating, and he looked pretty awful. Finally the king noticed his sad face and asked him what was wrong. My dad told him, "How can I smile when my hometown is in ruins?"

"Well," said the king. "what do you want me to do about it? How can I help?"

That was just the thing my dad needed to hear. He had all his plans ready, and he told the king he wanted time off to rebuild the walls of the city. He needed letters of safe passage, and wood, and people to work for him. Amazingly, the king granted all his requests.

So now we're off to Jerusalem. Sure, it'll be a great adventure, but I'm not happy about it. My dad talks about God, and he seems to be absolutely sure that this is God's plan.

But I'm not sure about that. Will God be any more real to me in Jerusalem than he is here in Babylon? I wonder—do I have to give up everything I love about my life to worship him?

Think About It: Are there things in your life that might stand between you and God, things that stop you from wanting to worship and love him?

Prayer: *Lord, you've given me many blessings: food, clothing, family, and school. Please help me to realize that they must not come between you and me. Keep me from worshiping things rather than you, my Savior. Amen.*

Checking Out the Walls

Read: Psalm 102:12-16

It's a long way from Babylon to Jerusalem. A long, long way.

We set off with the king's guard, plus letters to the rulers of the countries we would pass through. We stopped at several different places to pick up construction materials. By the time we got to Jerusalem, we were pretty loaded up.

I figured everyone would be very glad to see us when we arrived, but nobody even noticed. They must have seen the royal guard and figured we were Babylonian travelers.

The city was every bit as grubby and wrecked as my uncle Hanani had told us. With half the walls torn down, any old enemy could have walked right in to rob and plunder. Not that there was much to take. What a difference from Babylon, that hustling, bustling town filled with beautiful buildings and gardens and palaces!

My dad didn't make any grand announcement about his plans. He just quietly got us settled first. Then one night, he set off with a few men.

"I decided to inspect the walls, to see for myself what needs to be done," he explained to us the next morning at breakfast. "You know, our people here act as though there's no hope. It's time to change that. We can hold our heads up high, because we're God's chosen people. We don't need to be ashamed, because we have God on our side."

The next thing I knew, he'd visited the officials, the nobles, the priests, and anyone else who would listen, and had called them together for a meeting. A big crowd gathered, shuffling their feet and looking down at the ground, waiting for my father to say his piece. They looked like a sorry bunch, not at all like God's chosen people.

"Listen!" shouted my father. "I don't have to tell you what a mess this city is in. Our enemies Sanballat and Tobiah have managed to put a stop to the building program. But we can change that!

We can rebuild the walls so that our enemies will stop mocking us. Listen! You think I'm just telling you a fairy tale? No sir! This isn't just *my* idea . . . it's God's idea, and he's given his blessing to it." Then he told them about his prayer for the city and how God had answered that prayer by making the king gracious and helpful.

When the people heard that, they began to look interested. To tell you the truth, for the first time I was getting interested. We saw only rubble and a mess. My dad saw a beautiful city, one where God lived with his people. We were hearing only the mocking voices of our enemies, who wanted us to fail; but Dad was hearing God's voice, and God wanted us to succeed.

I began to see why my father loved this city so much, and why he had wanted to come back. Babylon was beautiful, but it was hard to find God there. The city was filled with fancy temples to heathen gods, but we could only worship the true God in back rooms and prayer closets. In Jerusalem there is one temple, to the one true God, and God lives right there with his people.

"So who will help?" asked my father, and the once-quiet crowd erupted in cheers.

"Yes, yes!" they said eagerly. "Let's get started."

It won't be long before our enemies will hear about this . . . but that's okay. Because we know who's on our side, and he will help us build his home.

Think About It: What causes you to get scared and quit working on the jobs God gives you? How can you get your courage back?

Prayer: *Lord, when people mock me and try to discourage me from doing my best, please speak louder than they do so I can hear you. I'd much rather work for you than for anyone else. Amen.*

Work and Prayer: Weapons Against the Enemy

Read: Psalm 125:1-2

Whenever something good happens, God's enemies get mad. They'll do whatever they can to mess up the good stuff.

The rebuilding of Jerusalem's walls was good stuff. When news of the project went through Israel, people came from all over to help make God's holy city a beautiful and safe place. They worked hard, with hope and joy in their hearts. So it wasn't long before Israel's enemies decided they'd better do something to stop the work.

First they tried using words as weapons. When Sanballat and Tobiah met people traveling to Jerusalem to help with the project, they'd say, "What on earth do you think you're doing? The job is hopeless: the walls are rubble, and everything is burned up." They'd stand outside the walls, watching us work and mocking us: "Those walls are so weak, a little bitty fox could knock them down. Give it up!"

Well, sticks and stones may hurt our bones, but that kind of talk couldn't touch us. The walls were half-built when our enemies tried another tactic. My dad and the other leaders heard of a plot to fight against the city—maybe not a big battle, but enough little attacks to get the workmen away from the walls and into the fight.

My father knew how to handle that threat too. We had a big prayer meeting to tell God about our troubles and to ask for his help. Then we posted guards to keep a lookout for sneak attacks, and everyone was sent back to work.

But Sanballat's and Tobiah's trashy talk and plans to attack us had gotten to some of our own people, and they began to whine and complain. "We're dog-tired. There's too much rubble—we'll never get the job done. Besides, what good are a few guards against Sanballat and his cronies? Our enemies are all around, waiting in the bushes for us. We're scared they're going to get us."

The discouragement began to spread through the town. Some of the workmen were ready to pack their bags and go back to the fields. But my dad said that if they began to think that way, they might as well have given up. It would mean the enemy had won without raising a sword.

And Dad just couldn't let that happen—not when he was sure that rebuilding the walls was God's plan. So he got organized. The workers were divided into two groups. One group would build while the other group would stand guard, armed to the teeth with bows and swords and spears. Then the builders could feel safe as they went about their work.

The other part of my father's plan was to remind the people what this work was all about. "Don't be afraid of them!" he urged the people. "Remember the Lord, who is great and awesome. Work and fight for your families, for your homes, and for God himself."

Did it work? It sure did! When you think of the greatness of God, the sneaky plans of little people just can't get you down.

The people went back to work, and the enemy slunk back home to try and think of new ways to harass us. And so it went, over and over again. They'd come up with new threats to stop the work, and the people of Israel, with God on their side, would fight back and keep working.

My dad kept a record of it all in his diary. Here's my favorite part: "So the wall was completed in fifty-two days. When all our enemies heard about this, all the surrounding nations were afraid, and lost their self-confidence, because they realized that this work had been done with the help of our God."

Hooray for God—and hooray for his people when they listen and obey!

Think About It: Our enemy the devil uses weapons like words, dangerous situations, discouragement, and fear to make sneak attacks on God's children. Has he made attacks on you with these weapons? How do you fight back?

Prayer: *God, help me realize that you are stronger than any attack the devil can make on me. Help me fight back with prayer and with your strength as my ally. Amen.*

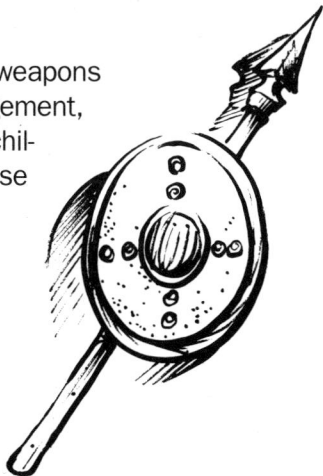

Party Time!

Read: Psalm 126:1-3

My dad loves to worship God. When we still lived in Babylon, he would go to his prayer room three times a day. He would kneel before the window that faced Jerusalem and pray, giving thanks to God for his blessings.

But I didn't always share my dad's joy. When we had worship times, I would whine, "Do I have to go to synagogue?" And my parents would look shocked and say, "Of course you do." But it's hard to worship a God who doesn't seem real to you.

I don't feel that way anymore, though. When we came back to Jerusalem, I began to sense that this was a special place. I saw how God protected us while we rebuilt his holy city. I felt his Spirit working in the people, and I began to realize that God was very, very real. And very, very awesome, and holy, and wonderful. And that he wants us to live with him.

So when Ezra the priest announced that there would be a special worship service after the walls were completed, I didn't whine and complain and say, "Do I have to go?" I said, "Count me in! I want to be there."

What a party that turned out to be! If you were old enough to understand what had happened, you were invited. Thousands and thousands of people gathered together at the new water gate. Ezra had built a big platform, and he stood on it with the other leaders so people could see them. We worshiped in a way we hadn't been able to for all our years of captivity—openly and joyously.

The Levites blew the ram's horn and showed the book of the law to the people. A shout of joy rose up, and then everything became very quiet as Ezra began to read. Every word was precious, and as we all listened, we were overcome by emotions. All around me, people were crying or bowing with their faces in the dust.

It's hard to describe that feeling. Maybe it is how people feel when they have been away from home for a long time. Finally, when they're back home, they realize how much they've missed the things that mean the most. They realize how much they have hurt their loved ones by staying away so long. I think that is how Israel felt about ignoring God's promises for so long. We realized how much we had hurt God by turning our backs to him, by not trusting him. And so we cried.

That's when my dad stood up and said, "Stop! Don't cry! This is a day of joy! This is party time—break open the best skins of wine, get out your fancy food, and rejoice! Invite your friends and neighbors to come, and give away your stuff to people who have nothing. Our God is a God of joy. The joy of the Lord is our strength!"

What a way to worship God! In the book of the law, we discovered that God had already told us how to party. It was called the Feast of Tabernacles, and we were supposed to go out into the hill, cut down branches and make leafy shelters for our families, living in them for a whole week. By doing that, we would remember our ancestors who had often lived in tents as they wandered in the wilderness. God had brought them to the promised land, just like he'd done with us now.

So we celebrated the feast. We cut down palm and olive branches and built little huts for ourselves on the flat roof of our house. We slept there every night under the stars. It was so much fun. Dad was right— our God is a God of joy.

Isn't it amazing that when we feel really, really sad and sorry for our sins, God comes to us and says, "Stand up! Rejoice! I've forgiven you, and you're free to be happy, to laugh, and to share your happiness with other people. In fact, that's what I want you to do . . . go out and share your joy."

Think About It: Is the joy of the Lord your strength? How can you share your joy with other people?

Prayer: *God, thank you for the gift of joy! Please help me share it with others. Amen.*

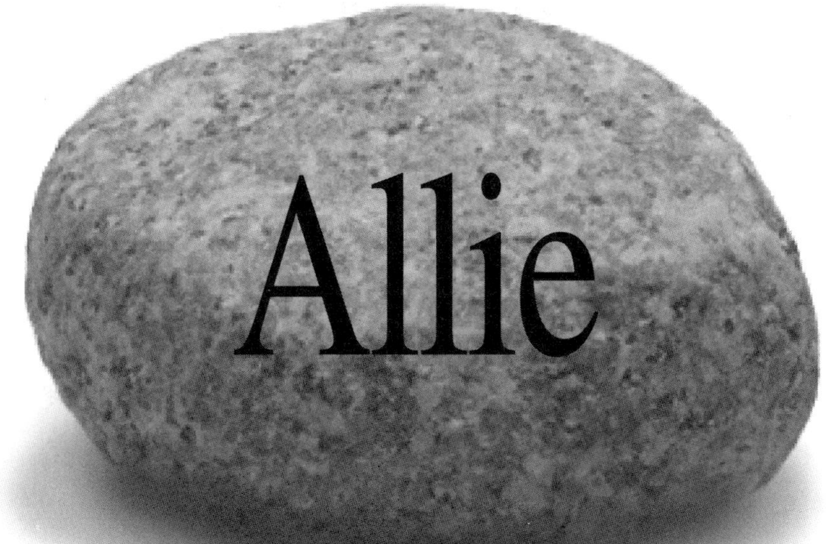
Allie

The First Day of School

Read: Psalm 20:1-5

The big yellow school bus stopped at the farm gate, and Allie jumped out. She ran down the drive and burst through the door. Her mom was sitting in front of the computer, her forehead wrinkled in concentration. Bills and papers were spread around the top of the desk.

"Oh my," said her mom, "I had no idea that school was over already. Well, tell me all about it—how did your first day of school go? Did Jenna from your church school class show you around?"

Allie's eyes were shining with excitement. "It was good, Mom—and yeah, Jenna showed me around, but I've got a new friend now. Her name's Shawna. We get to play baseball at recess, and Shawna's the captain of my team. She invited me to her birthday party next week. Can I go?"

Allie's mom smiled. "Whoa! Slow down!" she said. "I'm glad you had a good day, and yes, probably you may go to Shawna's party. Why don't we talk about it at supper when Dad's around? Meantime, would you go gather the eggs and do your other chores?"

Allie had a snack, put on her work jeans, and skipped out to the barn. Not even chores were going to get her down today. She felt like the luckiest girl alive.

The night before, Allie had hardly been able to eat her supper because she had been so nervous about the first day of school. Clint hadn't been much better. Leaving old friends and a neighborhood school was the pits.

Her dad had read Psalm 20 for family devotions. "May the LORD answer you when you are in distress," he had begun. Then he looked up at Clint and Allie and said with a grin, "It looks like this one was meant for you two!"

While her dad had continued reading aloud, Allie had remembered all the stories she'd read about King David. He'd sure had his bad days too. This psalm had been meant as a prayer before he went out to do battle.

"May he give you the desire of your heart," the psalm went on, and Allie had breathed a quick prayer: "Please, Lord, give me the desire of my heart—a good day at school."

Well, God had answered that prayer. He had helped her find a friend at this new school where she knew almost no one except Jenna from her church school class. Jenna was nice and had shown her around, but Shawna was special. And Shawna had picked her.

Shawna was so cool—she could have any friend she wanted, and she'd picked Allie! Shawna had hung around Allie all day, helping her get settled in her room, introducing her to the other kids, picking her for the baseball team. And inviting her to her birthday.

Fourth grade was going to be fun.

Think About It: What is "the desire of your heart" that you pray God will grant you?

Prayer: *Dear God, it is really awesome to know that you care about the desires of our hearts and that we can tell you all about them. Thank you for being a caring, loving God who wants us to be happy. Amen.*

The Second Day of School

Read: Psalm 20:6-9

When Allie came down for breakfast, she was surprised to see Dad and Uncle Charlie sitting at the table, sipping coffee. Usually they had breakfast early and were out inspecting the fields by the time she got up.

"It looks like the O-ring is shot," said Uncle Charlie. "I've had problems with that thing before."

"Whatever it is, we're stranded until it's fixed," said Dad wearily. "What a rotten thing to happen, just when the weather looks like it's in our favor." Then his face brightened when he saw Allie.

"Good morning, Allie-pally," he said with a grin. "If you hurry up and get ready, you can have a ride to school with me instead of taking the bus. Our harvester broke down, and I need to go into town to get a replacement part to fix it."

Allie rushed through her cereal and toast, then hopped into the car with Dad and Uncle Charlie. Getting to school early would be good—she could practice her baseball catching, and maybe Shawna would be there too.

"Farming is all new to me, Uncle Charlie," said Dad as he drove toward the school. "I just figured when the crops were ready we could harvest them. This breakdown gums up everything."

Uncle Charlie grinned. "Yeah, you're learning that things don't always go the way you expect them to. Rain and cold weather, equipment breakdowns, getting sick. . .you just can't count on smooth sailing. Farming is like life—sometimes there are bumps that upset you."

Dad smiled ruefully. He's probably thinking about the job he lost back in Chicago, thought Allie. It wasn't fair. And it didn't make sense. Just when it looked like things were going to work out for her, it looked like things were going wrong for her dad again.

Why wasn't God giving Dad the desires of *his* heart? Why wasn't the harvest going smoothly?

"Well," said Uncle Charlie, "it's like the good book says, like the Psalm you read last night: 'Some trust in John Deere tractors, and some in International Harvester equipment, but we trust in the name of God.'"

"It says that, does it?" said Dad with a grin. "I don't recall that the Bible said that, exactly. But you're right, Uncle. You can't count on a whole lot, but you can count on God to see you through it all. He hasn't let us down yet."

Allie sat thinking quietly the rest of the way to school. Moving from Chicago to Gold River was bad, but finding new friends was good. Losing a job was awful, but knowing God would take care of you, no matter what, was good.

Life doesn't always make sense, she thought—and yet, in an odd way, it does. I guess it's God who makes the difference.

Think About It: What doesn't make sense to you? How can believing in God make the difference?

Prayer: Dear Lord, help me not to trust in happiness that comes from money, or health, or my friends. Help me to put my trust in you, because you will never let me down. Amen.

The Third Day of School

Read: Psalm 25:4-7

The big yellow school bus pulled up to the farm gate, and Allie stumbled down the steps. Slowly she began walking up the long drive to the house.

Her feet dragged in the dust of the driveway, pushing up little puffballs around her ankles. On the first day of school, her shoes had been shiny and new. But now the grayish dust film made them appear old and beaten-up. Just like she felt.

She clumped up the verandah steps and pushed open the door. Her mom looked up with a smile from the computer desk where she was working.

"Hi, sunshine," she said. "How's it going?"

Allie shrugged her shoulders, dropped her backpack at the door, and headed for the stairs.

"Hey!" said her mom, surprised. "What's the matter?"

Allie turned toward her mom. "Why did we have to come to this place, anyway? Why couldn't Dad just find a job in Chicago?"

"Bad day, huh?" said her mom. "Would a cookie, some lemonade, and a shoulder rub help?"

Allie sat down at the kitchen table. Her mom set the snack down before her and began to knead Allie's shoulders. It felt good. Allie hadn't wanted to talk about the day, but the words came tumbling out.

"On Tuesday, Shawna invited me to her party, and now today she says she's only allowed to invite two kids. I was the last one she invited, so I can't go," she said. "And after she told me that, she basically acted like I wasn't alive, and she picked a new baseball team and I'm not on it, and nobody likes me at the school. I'm not going back. You can't make me."

Her mom didn't say anything, but she kept rubbing Allie's shoulders. The silence was driving Allie crazy. "I know what you told me," she said. "I know you said it takes time to make friends, and some friends are better than others, but I thought Shawna liked me."

Mom still kept quiet, and kept rubbing. "Yeah, and if I'd known Shawna was going to be like that, I wouldn't have trusted her," continued Allie. "I would have hung around with Jenna. She treated me nice the first day of school too, and showed me all around."

"And how did you treat Jenna's kindness?" asked her mom, rubbing a little harder.

"Ouch, that hurt, Mom," said Allie, and it wasn't only the back rub that hurt. Finding out the truth about herself was a little painful too.

Allie finished her lemonade and stood up. She had her chores to do, and that would give her some time to think. Maybe there was some way she could turn things around at school.

Maybe it wasn't too late to learn.

"Thanks for the back rub, Mom," she said. "And everything else too."

Think About It: Have you ever learned things about yourself you don't like very much? What did you do about it?

Prayer: *Dear Lord, long ago David prayed, "Show me your ways, O Lord, and teach me your paths. Guide me in your truth and teach me." You were with David; please be with me too. Amen.*

The Weekend

Read: Psalm 25:8-10

The sunshine streaming through the open curtains woke Allie. She stretched and yawned and stumbled to the window.

In the distance she could see the combine chugging away out in the fields, spitting golden streams of grain into the back of the truck. The flowers in the garden below, the birds singing in the trees—it all looked so good. Two days ago she'd told her mom that life was rotten. Now she felt lighthearted and happy. Yesterday had made the difference.

She thought back to yesterday. It had taken a lot of courage to get on the bus, knowing that Shawna was sitting back there with her friends, not caring how Allie felt. It had taken even more courage to walk over to the empty seat beside Jenna and ask if she could sit there.

Jenna had looked surprised, then smiled a little and nodded. Allie sat down, and for the first few miles they were both silent. Allie knew she had to say something—anything—but the words were stuck inside her mouth.

"Umm...uhh...like, I...I...like, I didn't know...uhh...sorry," she finally babbled. Jenna grinned at her.

"I should have warned you about Shawna when I showed you around school the first day," she said. "She treats everybody like that, pretending she's your best friend and then dropping you like a hot potato. You're not the first person it's happened to—she did it to me too."

Grateful, Allie smiled at Jenna. They had something in common, now, besides church school. They could both hate Shawna.

Maybe they could even make plans to pay her back for the way she had treated them.

But Jenna's next words surprised her. "I used to hate her, but now, in a weird way, I feel sorry for her. She's always jumping from friend to friend, like nobody is good enough. I wonder what would make her happy."

It wasn't a question Allie wanted to think about. It was more fun to keep a grudge.

Jenna continued, "I told Mr. Roberts, our church school teacher, about Shawna once, and he told me to pray for Shawna every night."

"So did it work? Is she nicer and happier now than she used to be?" asked Allie.

"Not really—not yet," said Jenna. "But I'm happier. It feels better to care about her than to be mad at her."

The girls chatted all the rest of the way to school. The long bus ride to and from school went faster than ever before.

And last night, before she went to bed, she decided to try what Jenna had suggested. She added Shawna to her list of people she asked God to bless. And Jenna was right. It felt better to care about Shawna than to be mad at her.

Think About It: Does keeping a grudge make anyone happy? What might be a better way to handle hurt feelings?

Prayer: *Lord, you instruct people in the way they should live. Your ways are loving and faithful. Please instruct me in ways that I need to be more loving and faithful. Amen.*

Reuben

Reuben Keeps Watch

Read: Acts 21:15-20

"Ma!" Reuben ran into the house. "Guess what, Ma? Guess who's come back to Jerusalem? Hardly anybody knows yet, but I saw him with my own two eyes." He danced excitedly around his mom, who was stirring soup over the fire.

Reuben's mom looked worriedly at her son. "Reuben," she warned, "if you've been sneaking around again where you shouldn't be. . . ."

"Come on, Ma," Reuben said indignantly. "I'm behaving myself, honest. I was hanging around the elder James's house when I saw this person. Now guess who it was, Ma."

Reuben's mom wasn't quite convinced of Reuben's innocence, but a slight smile played with the corners of her mouth as she dished the soup into bowls for the meal.

"If this person was at the elder James's house, and he's come back to town after a long stay away, and you know him well enough to recognize him, it must be . . . it's got to be . . . your Uncle Paul," she said.

"Right!" said Reuben happily, as he began sipping soup from his bowl. "He was walking down the road to James's house with about seven or eight other men, including that doctor, Luke, who travels with him. He saw me, Ma! He hugged me and told me to tell you he would come soon to see you."

Reuben's mom's face lit up. "Oh Reuben, that is good news." Then her face turned serious again. "It almost makes up for the disappointment I feel knowing my boy spends his days hanging out on the streets instead of at the synagogue, where he ought to be learning from the rabbi."

Reuben fidgeted and looked away. How was a guy supposed to tell his mom that it was awfully hard to listen to a boring old teacher when the sun was shining and the birds were singing outside the window? She just wouldn't understand.

He liked to explore Jerusalem: the shops and traders, the temple area, and the fortress Antonia, where the soldiers stayed and prisoners were kept. It livened up his boring life.

There was always the chance, too, that he might pick up a few scraps of food if he begged hard enough. That's what he'd been hoping for when he hung around James's house.

Ever since Dad had died, Mom had been depending on the food the deacons brought to their family every week. But famine and hardship had come to Jerusalem, and often Reuben felt like his backbone was pushing against his belly button. This soup he was eating—it was good, but there just wasn't enough of it.

But now Uncle Paul was back in town, and he was bringing a gift of money from the churches in Asia Minor. Good times were here again. God was taking care of his children.

Think About It: People were happy to see Paul back in Jerusalem. Who would you like to come to visit your school or church? Why?

Prayer: *Thank you, Lord, for faithful people who spread your love and good news wherever they go. Please help me to be one of those people, so that people are happy I'm around. Amen.*

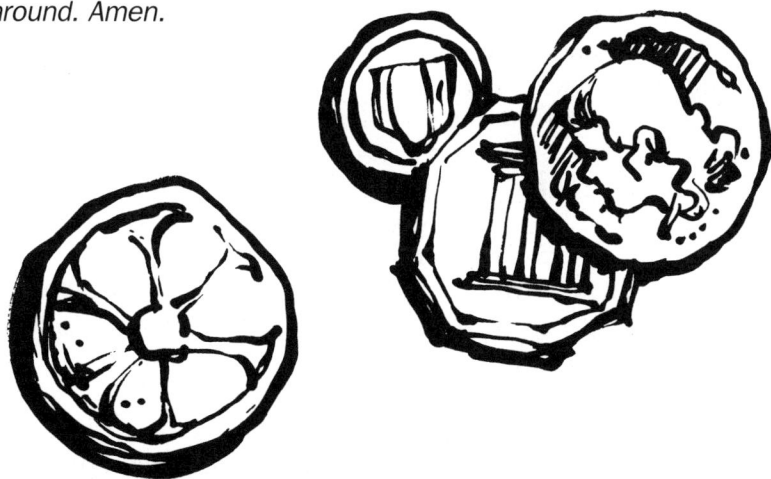

Going the Distance for God

Read: 1 Corinthians 15:58

"I guess I was just talking way too much," said Uncle Paul with a rueful grin, "and the room was hot and stuffy. The poor little fellow fell asleep and tumbled out the open window to the ground below."

"What happened to the boy?" asked Reuben's sister.

"I ran downstairs, threw myself on his body, and God used me to raise him from the dead," said Uncle Paul.

The children breathed a sigh of relief. Reuben and his younger brothers and sisters were sitting at Uncle Paul's feet, their eyes fixed on his face. When Uncle Paul told stories, you just had to listen. Reuben tried to picture what it must have been like to actually have lived in the stories Uncle Paul was telling.

He imagined himself with Uncle Paul in Thessalonica, where an angry crowd milled around the house where he was staying. He imagined himself and Uncle Paul being sneaked out of town in the dark. He imagined himself in Athens, standing with Uncle Paul on the steps of the Areopagus, the Greek court.

What a life that would be! Traveling, seeing things, getting into adventures and narrow escapes! Jerusalem was pretty tame compared to that. Reuben suddenly had an idea.

"Uncle Paul," he said urgently, "Uncle Paul, take me with you when you go the next time. I could help you, really I could. I could cook for you, and clean up after you, and run errands."

Uncle Paul smiled. "Reuben," he said, "it would surely be wonderful to have a helpful fellow like you with me. It's an offer I can hardly refuse."

Reuben's heart jumped excitedly.

"But . . . ," continued Uncle Paul.

Nuts! Grown-ups were so good at that, coming up with "ifs" and "buts."

Now Uncle Paul's face was serious. "Reuben, my life has not been easy. It's been lonely, dangerous, tiresome, and sometimes boring too. But that's not why I can't take you along. The real reason is that I won't be free to take you. Soon, I will become a prisoner."

Reuben's mom gasped and cried, "Oh, no!" Uncle Paul leaned over and hugged her. "Don't worry," he said. "God's Spirit is leading me and has shown me what will happen. I will be arrested and put in jail. But the Spirit also told me that it is part of God's plan for spreading the gospel to even more people. God will turn the bad into good, so praise him! He's in charge of my life."

Reuben gulped. Maybe it was a good thing Uncle Paul had declined his offer. He imagined what it would be like to spend day after day under arrest in a dirty, dingy cell. It wasn't a pretty or exciting picture.

Yet Uncle Paul seemed almost glad. Why? The question stayed with Reuben and gave him something to think about. Why? Why? Why?

Think About It: Why would Uncle Paul be glad to be in prison?

Prayer: *Lord, today we pray for people who are in prison because they are spreading the good news about Jesus. Please be very close to them and comfort them, and help them be glad. Amen.*

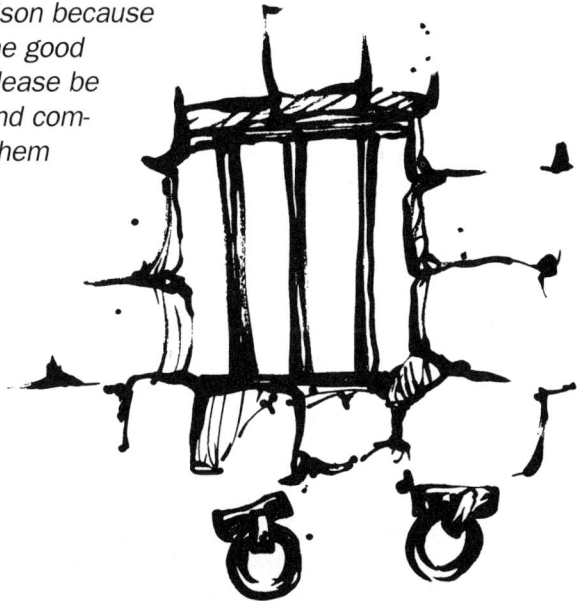

Reuben in the Crowd

Read: Acts 21:30-35

Reuben had good intentions about going to school, but, somewhere between home and the synagogue, he lost them. It was really Uncle Paul's fault, he told people later.

There he was, minding his own business, when he heard shouting and yelling. The sounds were coming from the temple area. And the temple wasn't in the same direction as the school. So what was a guy supposed to do?

Of course, he headed for the temple. By that time, crowds of people were running along the streets, rushing toward the temple as well. "Blasphemy! Traitor! Sinner!" they yelled, their fists pounding the air angrily.

One old man had to stop and catch his breath on a street corner. Reuben stopped too and said, "What's going on, sir? Why is everyone so angry?"

"They caught that sinner, Paul, that hypocrite and blasphemer. Haven't you heard? He brought a Greek into the Holy Temple. Everyone knows that's forbidden. The temple is only for God's chosen people. I hope they crucify him!" wheezed the old man indignantly.

Reuben's heart felt like ice in his chest. All these people wanted to kill Uncle Paul! Reuben had to do something to help him.

He pushed and shoved his way through the angry, noisy crowd, sometimes getting down on his haunches like a duck to squeeze between people's legs. And all the while he kept remembering Uncle Paul's words, "The Spirit has told me that I will be arrested." This was it! Maybe Uncle Paul would be thrown into a dungeon, and Reuben would never see him again.

Finally he got close enough to see what was happening. Dozens of men were punching and kicking at his uncle, who was crouched on the pavement, protecting his head with upraised arms. "Stop!"

shouted Reuben. "Stop it! He hasn't done anything wrong." But nobody heard.

Then a new sound rose above the shouting mass of people—the sound of Roman soldiers marching and commands being shouted. Suddenly, the crowd was quiet. At least two hundred soldiers were in and around the crowd, their swords drawn.

The commander grabbed Uncle Paul by the back of his neck and pulled him to his feet.

"Bind this man with two chains," he commanded a soldier. Then he turned to the crowd. "What's he done?"

Instantly, the shouting began again. "He's a devil!" shouted one. "He's a traitor!" shouted another. "Kill him! He deserves to die," they said, and more. The commander couldn't understand any of it. Finally, impatiently, he motioned for some soldiers to take Paul to the army barracks.

Reuben watched helplessly as the soldiers hoisted Uncle Paul high above their shoulders and marched to the Antonia fortress, close to the temple. He caught a glimpse of his uncle's bruised and battered face looking back at the crowd that wanted to kill him.

How could God turn something so bad into something good? It seemed impossible to Reuben. He wondered if Uncle Paul was still glad he'd come to Jerusalem.

Think About It: Is there any situation so bad that God can't make something good come out of it?

Prayer: *Lord God, it takes a lot of courage to stand firm when people are telling lies about you. Please give me that kind of courage in whatever situations I find myself. Amen.*

Paul Preaches to the Crowd

Read: Acts 21:40; Acts 22:1-3

Reuben watched as the soldiers carried his uncle away. He felt all mixed up inside. In one way, he was glad that the soldiers had rescued Uncle Paul from the people who were trying to kill him. But now Uncle Paul was headed for prison, for sure, for starting a riot. And it was anybody's guess whether he would ever get out of there.

Reuben supposed he'd have to go home and break the bad news to his mother. He turned to go, when suddenly the milling crowd became still and a voice rang out.

It was Uncle Paul! Reuben turned to see what was going on.

"Brothers and fathers, listen to my defense," Paul began.

What?! Brothers and fathers?! The people in this angry mob were Uncle Paul's enemies, not his loving family. How could Uncle Paul call them brothers? Why did he need to defend himself against their lies?

He was standing on the steps leading up to the fortress. Ringed around him were Roman soldiers with their Commander Claudius Lysias. And stretched out over the whole temple square was the crowd, quiet and ready to listen to Uncle Paul's defense against their accusations.

Then Uncle Paul began to tell his story . . . how he'd been brought up in a good family . . . how he'd studied with the Pharisees, and was eager to do God's will . . . how he'd thought that Christians were rebels and sinners and joined the posses that hunted them down. Even how he took a trip to Damascus so he could take Christians prisoner there.

"Good for you," muttered a man beside Reuben. Others nodded their heads in approval.

And then Uncle Paul told the story of how Jesus had appeared to him on the road to Damascus, and how his life had turned around.

Even though Reuben had heard this story many times before, he was still held spellbound. Uncle Paul sure knew how to tell a good story, and this was the best story of all—how Jesus, the son of God, was real, and how he still wanted people to follow him.

Miracles still happen, thought Reuben. Minutes ago, it looked like Uncle Paul was headed for disaster. Reuben had wondered how God could turn something bad into something good; yet here, right before his eyes, something very good was happening.

Thousands of people, including soldiers and priests and Pharisees, were listening to Paul's preaching. They were hearing the wonderful story of Jesus, maybe for the very first time. They had seen that, even though they had treated Paul very badly, he'd called them his brothers and had been respectful of them.

"Go for it, Uncle Paul," Reuben cheered silently, and said a prayer of thanks for miracles.

Think About It: Have you ever had a time when something you thought was impossible actually happened?

Prayer: *God, you are so very good. Thank you for your miracles every day, some little, some big. Open my eyes so that I can see and recognize them. Amen.*

Reuben Visits Jail

Read: Luke 11:9-10

Reuben had never been in jail before, and he sure didn't like it. It was dark and smelly and filled with the sounds of prisoners moaning and screaming. But Reuben swallowed his fear as he followed the guard. He reminded himself that he could do this for Uncle Paul.

Earlier, Reuben had watched in horror as the quiet crowd listening to Paul's sermon had suddenly become angry when Paul said that Jesus had come to save Gentiles as well as Jews. They'd screamed, "Get rid of him!" and tried to snatch him from the soldiers. The commander had gotten him into the fortress just in time.

Reuben wanted to do something—anything—to help his uncle. So he told the guards he was Paul's servant and that he wanted to bring food and medicine to his master. They'd actually let him in! Now the guard opened the thick door to his uncle's cell.

Reuben wanted to run to his uncle and hug him, hard. Instead, he bowed before him and said, "Sir, I've come to bring you some food and medicine, and to take your orders for any tasks you want me to do while you are here."

"Ahh," said Paul. For just a second his eyes twinkled with understanding. "You're a good and faithful . . . servant—an answer to prayer!"

The guard snorted and rolled his eyes. "Your answer to prayer can only stay a few minutes," he said with a snarl, then backed out of the jail cell, closing the door behind him.

Paul and Reuben hugged hard. "Did they hurt you, Uncle Paul?" asked Reuben anxiously. "Did they whip you?"

"They had me tied up and ready to flog," replied Paul. Reuben gasped. "But then I asked them whether it was legal to whip a Roman citizen who hasn't been found guilty of anything, and they backtracked really quickly. Being a Roman citizen is good protection.

"Instead of giving me a whipping, they're going to turn me over to the Sanhedrin, the Jewish court. The Pharisees and Sadducees are going to put me on trial."

"Uncle Paul, I don't think those guys in the Sanhedrin like you very well," said Reuben anxiously. "They're going to try and trap you into saying something that will put you back in jail. What are you going to say to them? How will you answer their questions?"

"I'm really not too worried," said his uncle. "Do you believe in Jesus, Reuben?"

"Yeah, but . . . yeah, I do, but Jesus isn't here to speak for you now, Uncle Paul," said Reuben. "You have to do it yourself."

"Ahh, but he is here, Reuben," answered Paul. "Before he went to heaven, he told his followers not to worry if they had to go to court, that the Holy Spirit would speak through us. So I'm not going to lie awake all night writing a speech, Reuben. Jesus has the speech all written for me, and I just have to give it."

They heard the guard's footsteps in the hall and his keys jingling in the lock. Paul and Reuben let go of each other.

"So tell my brother James what I've told you. He'll know what to do," Paul said in his best boss-to-servant voice as the guard entered the cell. "And boy, you come back here in two days for more orders. Do you hear?"

"Yes sir," Reuben said as he bowed once more, a humble servant of his Uncle Paul—and of Jesus too.

Think About It: Is it scary to talk about Jesus to people who don't know him? Who will help you?

Prayer: *Lord, I confess that sometimes I don't talk about you when I should because I'm scared people will make fun of me or ridicule me. Forgive me, Lord. Help me to speak up the next time I have the chance. Amen.*

Reuben Overhears a Scary Secret

Read: 1 Peter 4:12-16

Late the next day, Reuben paced about outside the temple courts, listening to shouts and angry voices coming from inside the building.

His Uncle Paul was standing before seventy of the most important men in Jerusalem, answering their charges. These powerful officials could ask King Herod to put Paul to death if they decided he had broken a very serious law.

And people had accused him of a very serious crime. They had said that Uncle Paul had taken a Greek person inside the temple. Breaking the law forbidding that was punishable by death. The law was even written on the stones of the courtyard.

All around town, Christians were meeting in prayer. But Reuben was too nervous and restless to sit and pray. Instead, he walked and prayed. "Please! Please, God, listen," he silently begged as he walked back and forth. "Let him say the right things."

Suddenly, the doors burst open, and Reuben could see a crowd of people inside, yelling and raising their fists. "He's innocent!" shouted a stately looking Pharisee, while from the other side of the room a red-faced Sadducee tore at his clothes and screamed, "Guilty! Guilty! Guilty!"

Through the crowd came a knot of soldiers protecting their prisoner, Paul. "Let's get him out of here before they tear him apart," shouted the commander. Uncle Paul looked awfully small and helpless as he was hustled out. Reuben's heart sank. Uncle Paul was going back to jail.

Then he noticed a group of men, their faces ugly with anger, pushing their way through the doorway. "I don't believe it!" exclaimed one of them. "How can those rulers be so blind? Can't they see he's guilty?"

Reuben crept behind a pillar so the men wouldn't see him.

"We can't let this happen," said a second voice. "If they won't punish Paul, then someone else should take care of it."

"Well spoken, Zeb," said another. "We know how to take care of him, don't we?"

"Look, let's not talk here," said the first man, lowering his voice. "Let's meet at the shop of Joseph the stonemason in a few hours and make plans."

"Spread the word," added Zeb, as the men began moving away. "There's strength in numbers."

As the men moved away, Reuben jumped out from behind the pillar. He had to do something, but he didn't know exactly what. Should he follow the men and find out more about their plans? That could be dangerous, and his mom would not be happy with him if he weren't home for supper.

Perhaps, instead, he should tell the commander of the guard what he had heard. But the commander of the guard was a busy man, especially now. He might not even listen to a little Hebrew kid, and if he listened, would he believe that the grumbles of a few men should be taken seriously?

Reuben watched the men beginning to disappear down the courtyard steps. He really had no choice, but he was so frightened his knees were knocking together. Was it just a few days ago that he'd been thinking Jerusalem was boring? He'd wanted adventure, but he hadn't realized how scary adventure could be! If only he had someone big and strong with him to protect him.

Wait! He did have someone big and strong with him. "Please, God, protect me. I'm counting on you," he prayed as he hurried across the pavement, keeping the men in sight.

Think About It: What hard choices have you had to make recently? How do you make a decision when you have to choose between two things?

Prayer: *Dear God, I wish I didn't have to make tough choices. Please give me a clear mind when I'm not sure what to do. Teach me to count on you to help me, because I am weak but you are strong. Amen.*

Goodbye, Fear—
Hello, Power

Read: Isaiah 43:1-3a

Once again, Reuben was walking behind the guard down the jail corridor, listening to the screams and moans of prisoners who lived behind closed doors with no hope of escape. Today he knew what those prisoners felt like. His heart was filled with despair.

As soon as they were alone together, Reuben threw himself into his uncle's arms.

"They're going to kill you," he sobbed. "There's nothing you can do about it. They're going to get you, and I'm so scared I'll never see you again."

Gently, Paul led Reuben to a stool. "You're wrong, Reuben, nobody is going to kill me yet," he said. He spoke with such certainty that Reuben stopped crying and looked up in surprise. "God still has plans for me. Now tell me what this is all about."

Reuben dried his eyes and began: "I heard some men plan to kill you, Uncle Paul," he said. "I knew they were going to meet at Joseph the stonemason's shop, so I hid behind some rocks and rubble to hear their plans. They never knew I was there, and I came here as fast as I could when they left."

For a moment, he smiled, recalling the feeling he had of being Jesus' partner in that dusty shop. Then he remembered his bad news and swallowed hard.

"Uncle Paul, there are forty men who have sworn an oath that they will not eat or drink until you are dead!" Reuben gulped and went on. "They have asked the chief priest to request that you come to the Sanhedrin tomorrow. The men will be waiting for you to be brought out, and then they will ambush the soldiers and kill you. There are more than forty of them, Uncle Paul, and there will only be a few soldiers guarding you. You don't have a chance."

"You did well, Reuben," said Paul. "Coming here was the right thing. I'm sure it was part of God's plan that you overheard those men. I know they won't succeed, because listen: last night, when I was just about as scared and tired as you were, God spoke to me.

"He said, 'Take courage! Just as you have witnessed about me here in Jerusalem, so you must also testify about me in Rome!' So you see, those men made plans, but God has made better plans, and God will always win out. You're going to be God's partner in making sure that Rome hears the gospel too."

Paul embraced Reuben tightly. "You'll have to tell the commander what you told me, but don't be frightened, Reuben. Remember, you're on God's side. You can't have a better partner than that."

Soon Reuben was following the guard back down the hallway on his way to speak to the commander of the fortress. He wondered how his feelings could have changed so quickly from fear to excitement. That's what happens when you become God's partner, he thought. If God's got plans for you, nothing is going to get in the way. That's pretty awesome.

Think About It: Is it possible that God has plans for you too? What might those plans be? How can you be God's partner in those plans?

Prayer: *Dear God, I'd like to be your partner in whatever plans you have for me. Please help me to not be frightened and to dare to do great things for you. Amen.*

A Letter from Caesarea

Read: Matthew 28:16-20

Dear Reuben,

Greetings to you! May God bless you and keep you.

How very glad I was that you told your story to Claudius, the garrison's commander. It must have taken a lot of courage to follow those men and listen to their plans, but by doing that you saved my life! I thank God for such a wonderful nephew.

Those zealots who planned to kill me had made up a pretty good plot, but Claudius was smarter than they. As soon as he heard your story, he came to me. He said, "Your nephew's story is no fairy tale. I just received a request from the Sanhedrin to bring you before them tomorrow. I've agreed to do that, but don't worry. Before tomorrow comes, you'll be out of here."

That night he rounded up hundreds of troops on horseback. They snuck me away in the middle of the night while all the plotters were sleeping soundly in their beds. I would have liked to have seen their faces when they woke up the next morning and found out I wasn't in the city anymore. I wonder if they kept their oath not to eat or drink until I'm dead. If so, they must be pretty hungry and thirsty by now!

They may be starving, but I'm doing fine. Felix, the governor, is treating me well here, allowing my friends to come and go freely to bring food and to visit with me. I have had so many opportunities to talk about Jesus that I'm almost thankful I'm in jail! As people come to love Jesus through my ministry here, I trust God more and more. His ways are perfect, and he's taking care of me.

Let me give you an example. About five days after I arrived, Ananias the high priest showed up with some other people from the Sanhedrin and a lawyer by the name of Tertullus. I had to appear before Felix, who's in charge here, to answer to their accusations. Tertullus is a big bag of wind; his speech went on and on. He said I stirred up riots—and you know yourself, Reuben, that all I did was go to the temple to worship. He said I tried to dishonor the temple by bringing a non-Jew into it. In the end, he couldn't come up with any real crime that I'd committed. Felix sent them all home empty-handed.

Governor Felix is an interesting character. He knows about the way of Jesus because he is married to Drusilla, who is a Hebrew like we are. He's sent for me several times already, asking me questions about my beliefs. Every time I talk to him he's surrounded by friends and servants, so my witness reaches many people. I'm happy to say that there are now other Christians in the court of Felix the governor, people who have heard my testimony and have believed.

Felix himself and Drusilla his wife are not believers yet. I think they're scared that if they believe, they'll have to give up some of their private sins. They don't realize that when they believe, they'll finally be free from the sin that holds them prisoner.

Think of it, Reuben! I'm in jail, yet I'm free, because I'm no longer a slave to sin. The governor and his wife, even though they live in a fancy palace, are shackled like common prisoners by their sins. Perhaps someday they'll finally give in to God, like I did, and give their lives to him. Pray for it, Reuben, and for me too, and for all Christians who spread good news in foreign lands. And pray that I'll have the opportunity to do the same in Rome.

Grace and peace to you.

Love from your Uncle Paul.

Think About It: Do you have some private sins that are tying you up in knots? How can Jesus help set you free?

Prayer: *Lord, I thank you for coming to earth to set people free from their sins. I thank you that no matter where we are, whether in jail, or in dangerous places, or far from home, you are there too, and have plans for us. Amen.*